S0-AZP-365

Social Issues
in Literature

Slavery in
Narrative of the Life
of Frederick Douglass

Other Books in the Social Issues in Literature Series:

Social Issues
in Literature

Slavery in
Narrative of the Life
of Frederick Douglass

Claudia Durst Johnson, Book Editor

GREENHAVEN PRESS
A part of Gale, Cengage Learning

GALE
CENGAGE Learning·

Farmington Hills, Mich • San Francisco • New York • Waterville, Maine
Meriden, Conn • Mason, Ohio • Chicago

Elizabeth Des Chenes, *Director, Content Strategy*
Douglas Dentino, *Manager, New Product*

© 2014 Greenhaven Press, a part of Gale, Cengage Learning

WCN: 01-100-101

Gale and Greenhaven Press are registered trademarks used herein under license.

For more information, contact:
Greenhaven Press
27500 Drake Rd.
Farmington Hills, MI 48331-3535
Or you can visit our Internet site at gale.cengage.com

ALL RIGHTS RESERVED.
No part of this work covered by the copyright herein may be reproduced, transmitted, stored, or used in any form or by any means graphic, electronic, or mechanical, including but not limited to photocopying, recording, scanning, digitizing, taping, Web distribution, information networks, or information storage and retrieval systems, except as permitted under Section 107 or 108 of the 1976 United States Copyright Act, without the prior written permission of the publisher.

For product information and technology assistance, contact us at

Gale Customer Support, 1-800-877-4253
For permission to use material from this text or product, submit all requests online at
www.cengage.com/permissions

Further permissions questions can be emailed to permissionrequest@cengage.com

Articles in Greenhaven Press anthologies are often edited for length to meet page requirements. In addition, original titles of these works are changed to clearly present the main thesis and to explicitly indicate the author's opinion. Every effort is made to ensure that Greenhaven Press accurately reflects the original intent of the authors. Every effort has been made to trace the owners of copyrighted material.

Cover image © Everett Collection Historical/Alamy.

LIBRARY OF CONGRESS CATALOGING-IN-PUBLICATION DATA

Slavery in Narrative of the Life of Frederick Douglass / Claudia Durst Johnson, book editor.
    pages cm. -- (Social Issues in Literature)
    Summary: "Social Issues in Literature: Slavery in Narrative of the Life of Frederick Douglass: This series brings together the disciplines of sociology and literature. It looks at a work of literature through the lens of the major social issue that is reflected in it"-- Provided by publisher.
    Includes bibliographical references and index.
    ISBN 978-0-7377-6986-9 (hardback) -- ISBN 978-0-7377-6987-6 (paperback)
    1. Douglass, Frederick, 1818-1895--Juvenile literature. 2. African American abolitionists--Biography--Juvenile literature. 3. Abolitionists--United States-- Biography--Juvenile literature. 4. Slaves--United States--Biography--Juvenile literature. 5. Slavery--United States--History--Juvenile literature. 6. Slavery in literature--Juvenile literature. 7. Social ethics in literature--Juvenile literature. 8. Douglass, Frederick, 1818-1895. Narrative of the life of Frederick Douglass, an American slave. I. Johnson, Claudia Durst, 1938- compiler of edition.
    E449.S675 2014
    973.8092--dc23
    [B]

    2013047318

Printed in Mexico
1 2 3 4 5 6 7 18 17 16 15 14

Contents

Chapter 3: Contemporary Perspectives on Slavery in the United States

Introduction

On Wednesday, June 19, 2013, 168 years after the publication of *Narrative of the Life of Frederick Douglass*, the leaders of the United States Senate and the House of Representatives met in the Capitol's Emancipation Hall to unveil a seven-foot, 1,700-pound statue of an African American. The statue was in honor of Frederick Douglass, who his great-great-granddaughter described as a fighter for freedom and equality for "all of us." He had been, of course, a slave himself, as well as one of the most courageous and effective voices for the abolition of slavery and an advisor to President Abraham Lincoln.

What was this institution of slavery that Frederick Douglass put himself at such risk to eliminate? A type of servitude, known as indentured white slavery, was part of settlement culture in the New World upon the arrival of the first English and Europeans, even before African slaves were brought to North American shores. The two had a few things in common. Over the course of the servitude—the length of which was determined by legal documents signed by the servant or his or her relative—they were beaten, given squalid living conditions and inadequate food, overworked, forbidden to leave, and tracked down and hauled back to their masters when they did try to escape. However, the differences between indentured servitude and slavery were momentous: Black slaves had been captured against their wills, were regarded as chattel, and were thrown into a culture foreign from their own. They had not sold themselves, as indentured servants had, for a specific time period after which they would be free. Except in extremely rare cases, slaves were slaves until they died. Furthermore, it was decreed by law that the descendants of slaves would be the property of their masters forever. Since the labor of slaves was so monetarily lucrative, they were bred like animals. Each new slave child born would soon be a laborer without pay for the master or a valuable piece of property to be sold.

The context of slavery in the United States is essential in historically placing *Narrative of the Life of Frederick Douglass* in perspective. The first recorded instance of Africans being brought to America was in 1619. Not long after, one of the many laws passed in the colonies to strengthen slavery dictated that slaves and their progeny would be slaves in perpetuity. In 1818, the probable year of Frederick Douglass's birth, slavery on North American soil was a 209-year-old institution.

The United States Declaration of Independence indicated that "all men are created equal," but this had nothing to do with slaves, women, and those without property, none of whom had the right to vote. From 1777 to 1804, many northern states and western territories abolished slavery. However in 1793, in a bargain with southern states, Congress enacted the Fugitive Slave Law, whereby slaves who escaped to free states could still be hunted down and returned to their owners. In 1807 Congress banned the importation of slaves. This was roughly the national situation when Douglass was born.

When Douglass was a teenager and was educating himself, the abolitionist movement, established by William Lloyd Garrison, along with Arthur and Lewis Tappan, was underway. In 1831 a revolt orchestrated by a slave, Nat Turner, was brutally put down and caused the South to pass harsher slave codes, making it even more difficult for Douglass to continue his education and to educate other slaves.

The Fugitive Slave Law had been reinforced when Douglass escaped to New York when he was in his twenties. Nevertheless, he exposed himself to danger when he became a public lecturer for the cause of abolition and as the author of *Narrative* in 1845. He fled to England to avoid capture. English friends purchased his freedom, and Douglass felt it was safe for him to return to the United States. Fourteen years later, the Civil War was fought over slavery, and in December 1865, slavery was abolished in the United States with the addition of the Thirteenth Amendment to the Constitution.

Chronology

1818

Frederick Bailey is born in Talbot County, Maryland.

1825

Douglass's mother, who was separated from him when he was a baby, visits him for the last time before she dies.

1826

Douglass is sent to live with the Hugh Auld family in Baltimore, Maryland, where he teaches himself to read.

1831

William Lloyd Garrison starts an abolitionist newspaper, the *Liberator*, in Boston.

1833

Douglass is returned to rural Maryland after the death of his master who he once suspected was his father. Garrison, along with Arthur and Lewis Tappan, establish the American Anti-Slavery Society.

1834

Douglass's presumed rebellious behavior prompts his master to send him to Edward Covey, a slave breaker. When Covey cannot "break" him, Douglass is sent to work for another man.

1836

Douglass and several other young men attempt an escape, which fails. He is sent back to the Hugh Auld family in Baltimore, where he learns a trade, turning over most of his money to Auld.

1838

Douglass escapes to New York City and is married to a free black woman whom he knew in Baltimore. They move to New Bedford, Massachusetts, where he works on the docks.

1841

Douglass meets William Lloyd Garrison, founder of the abolitionist movement. For four years, Douglass lectures for the anti-slavery society throughout the Northeast and Midwest.

1842

The Supreme Court upholds the Fugitive Slave Law.

1845

Douglass publishes *Narrative of the Life of Frederick Douglass.* Fearing capture, he leaves for England.

1846

Friends in England buy Douglass from Auld for $750, and he becomes a free man.

1847

Douglass returns to the United States where he starts his own newspaper in Buffalo, New York.

1848

Douglass attends the first women's rights convention at Seneca Falls, New York, and speaks in support of the radical idea of women's suffrage.

1855

Douglass publishes *My Bondage and My Freedom.*

1859

John Brown and his followers attack the arsenal at Harper's Ferry. Douglass, a friend of Brown's who did not approve of the attack, is accused of complicity and again flees to England. However, he returns upon the death of his daughter.

1861–1865
Throughout the Civil War, Douglass serves as an advisor to President Abraham Lincoln.

1865
The Thirteenth Amendment banning slavery throughout the United States becomes part of the Constitution.

1881
Douglass publishes *The Life and Times of Frederick Douglass.*

1889
President Benjamin Harrison appoints Douglass minister resident and consul-general to the Republic of Haiti and charge d'affaires to Santo Domingo.

1891
Douglass moves to Anacostia Heights in the District of Columbia.

1895
Douglass dies.

Background on
Frederick Douglass

From Slavery to National Prominence

Russell K. Hively

Russell K. Hively is a teacher in Neosho, Missouri.

The following viewpoint tells the phenomenal history of Frederick Douglass; from slavery he rose to prominence as an advisor to US presidents, as US minister to Haiti, as a speaker, as the author of several books, and as the founder and editor of a newspaper. He was born of a slave mother he rarely saw and of a father whose identity he never knew. He and other young slave children, who were kept in pens with dogs and pigs, wearing only filthy shirts, were called pigs and often starved. As adults, they were beaten. Nevertheless, through subterfuge and trickery, Douglass learned to read and write with sophistication and to master elegant oratory.

Champion of the suppressed people of the world, Frederick Douglass was an escaped slave who rose to become the United States minister to Haiti and a counselor to four presidents. A man with no formal education who spoke at universities all over the world, Douglass, who as a youngster slept in an animal pen, eventually became wealthy enough to afford the home of his dreams.

Douglass's Early Childhood as a Slave

Frederick Augustus Washington Bailey was born in Tuckahoe, Maryland, which he once described as "a small district of country, thinly populated, and remarkable for nothing I know of more than the worn-out sandy, desert-like appearance of its

Russell K. Hively, "Frederick Douglass," "Afro-American Writers Before the Harlem Renaissance," *Dictionary of Literary Biography*, ed. Trudier Harris and Thadious M. Davis, vol. 50, 1986. Copyright © 1986 Cengage Learning.

soil." He calculated his birth date to have been in February 1817; later in life, he celebrated it on 14 February. His mother, Harriet Bailey, was a literate slave; his father is presumed to have been a white man. During the first few years of his life he was raised by his grandparents, Betsey and Isaac Bailey. "My only recollections of my own mother are of a few hasty visits made in the night on foot, after the daily tasks were over. . . . Of my father I know nothing. Slavery had no recognition of fathers, as none of families." Betsey Bailey was held in high esteem by her owner, and her only job was the raising of the youngsters whose mothers were working in the fields.

Douglass's master was Capt. Aaron Anthony, who owned several farms in Tuckahoe and was chief clerk and butler on the home plantation of Col. Edward Lloyd. After a few years Douglass was marched from his grandmother's cabin to the main plantation where he was put into a breeding pen with dogs and pigs, where the smaller children were kept. Some of the children in the pen with Douglass were his brothers and sisters. They were called "pigs," and their main fare was corn mush, which they dipped from a trough with oyster halves or pieces of old shingle. Frederick's overseer in the pen was a . . . woman called Aunt Katy. The young Bailey had one long tow-linen cloth shirt which hung to his knees. He wore this garment day and night, and it was washed once a week.

First Steps Toward Freedom: Learning to Read

Frederick's first work was to serve as errand boy to Lucretia Auld, a daughter of Colonel Lloyd. In January 1826 he was sent to Baltimore, Maryland, to Hugh Auld, brother-in-law of Lucretia, to care for the Aulds' "bright-eyed and beloved boy Tommy." Although Frederick was picked on by the boys in the city and he disliked being locked away from the out-of-doors, he was treated by Hugh's wife Sophia with dignity. Freddy (her nickname for him) became like a stepbrother to little

Tommy. Hugh Auld was not as congenial, but he was completely wrapped up in his shipbuilding and left Frederick under the care of his wife. At young Bailey's request Sophia began teaching him how to read. He soon learned the alphabet and could spell words three and four letters long. When Sophia told her husband of Frederick's accomplishment, he forbade her from teaching the boy anymore. He told her, "If you give a n----- an inch, he will take an ell. . . . If he learns to read the Bible, it will forever unfit him to be a slave."

Frederick invented his own ways of learning to read. Having earned a little money by blacking boots for some gentlemen, he purchased a copy of *The Columbian Orator,* which he used not only to improve his reading but to learn the principles of freedom from the speeches included in the book. He soon began to read the daily newspaper, the *Baltimore American,* and learned of the abolition movements in the North. This new knowledge fueled his desire to be free.

When Frederick was put to work running errands for the workers in the shipyards, he saw the carpenters writing the location of certain boards on the new ships. The boy traced the markings and in this manner taught himself to write. He often tricked neighborhood boys into writing contests as a way to get them to aid in his lessons. Later, when Tommy was going to school, Frederick was frequently left at home alone, and he used Tommy's books to practice his reading and writing skills.

In 1833 he returned to St. Michaels, Maryland, and to Thomas Auld, his new owner after Colonel Anthony's death. Young Bailey, who was beginning to show signs of independent thinking, was put in charge of "Mr. Thomas's" horse, an outlaw that constantly ran away. Neither the horse nor the boy was broken by beatings, and on 1 January 1834 Bailey was placed in the care of Edward Covey, a man paid to break disrespectful slaves. Covey enjoyed sneaking up on the slaves to see if he could catch them doing anything worthy of a beating. For his stealthiness, he earned the nickname "the snake." Covey put Bailey to work in the fields, where he was an awkward hand. He was beaten three days after he arrived and for over one year was beaten at least once a week with either a stick or a piece of cowskin. . . .

A First Attempt at Freedom

In 1836, with five others, Henry Harris, John Harris, Sandy Jenkins, Charles Toberts, and Henry Bailey, Frederick Bailey began forming a scheme for escape. They planned to steal a canoe and row up the Chesapeake Bay to the North. Frederick wrote passes for each of them, and they planned to escape on Easter eve. Their escape was thwarted, and they were dragged fifteen miles behind horses to jail. Bailey was never convicted but was sent back to Hugh Auld in Baltimore.

There Bailey was hired out by Auld to William Gardiner to learn to caulk ships, but the white workers refused to work with Bailey because he was black, and he was forced to quit. He then went to work for Walter Price and received the highest caulker's wages, up to $9 a week, which he was forced to turn over to Auld. Having to hand over his money convinced Bailey he had to escape. He first acquired partial freedom by hiring himself out and paying a weekly fee to Auld. This arrangement required him to live on his own and provide his own keep. Once, when he did not make a payment on time, he was called back to Auld's care.

On Monday, 3 September 1838, with the moral and financial support of freedwoman Anna Murray, he left Baltimore and slavery. He obtained papers resembling those of a free sailor, and he boarded a train in disguise. After a one-day stopover in Philadelphia, he reached New York. "I soon found that New York was not quite so free or so safe a refuge as I had supposed, and a sense of loneliness and insecurity again oppressed me most sadly." He feared being recaptured by the many slave hunters in New York, and he was lucky to befriend a sailor who took him to David Ruggles, the secretary of the New York vigilance committee and the local underground railroad agent. While Bailey was hiding with Ruggles, Anna Murray came from Baltimore, and they were married 15 September 1838 by Presbyterian minister J.W.C. Pennington. Ruggles relocated the newlyweds to New Bedford, Massachusetts. They sailed on the *John W. Richmond* to their new home. . . .

Douglass's Introduction to the Abolitionist Movement

After living in New Bedford for a few months, he was approached by a young man who asked him to subscribe to William Lloyd Garrison's *Liberator*. Douglass said the "paper took a place in my heart second only to the Bible." In summer of 1841 Douglass attended an antislavery convention that was held in Nantucket under the direction of Garrison and his friends. William C. Coffin, who had heard Douglass speak to some friends at a church in New Bedford, sought Douglass out and asked him to say a few words at the convention. Douglass spoke of some of the things he had seen as a slave. In response to his speech, a contemporary wrote, "your whole soul was fired." At the close of the convention, John A. Collins, the general agent of the Massachusetts Anti-Slavery Society, solicited Douglass to become an agent for his organization. Although he feared he might be discovered by his owners, he agreed to act as an agent for a three-month period. "Fugitive slaves were rare then, and as a fugitive slave lecturer, I had the advantage of being a 'bran new fact.'" His strong, pleasant speaking voice helped turn the three months into four years.

During his four years of work for the society, Douglass suffered from many prejudices. When his troupe traveled on trains, he was forced to ride in the Negro or Jim Crow car. Sometimes his white campaigners would join him, but he felt they should take advantage of the accommodations they had. . . .

From Fugitive to Freedom

In 1845 he wrote the stories of his life as he had been telling them in his orations. The result was *Narrative of the Life of Frederick Douglass*. This simple narration became a best seller on two continents and was translated into both French and German. It was a small volume of 125 pages selling for fifty cents with introductions by Garrison and [abolitionist Wendell] Phillips. The book came off the press in May 1845. "Considered merely as a narrative," read a review in the *New York Tribune*, "we never read one more simple, true, coherent, and warm with genuine feeling. It is an excellent piece of writing, and on that score to be prized as a specimen of powers of the black race, which prejudice persists in disputing."

After his *Narrative* was published Douglass, for fear of being recaptured, fled to England. He was given a second-class cabin ticket but in time had almost free run of the *Cambria*. Only once was there trouble, and that was when he was going to speak about slavery on invitation of the ship's captain. Some passengers from Georgia attempted to prevent his speaking but were rewarded for their efforts by being put into irons. Douglass spent two years lecturing in England, Ireland, Scotland, and Wales, and he corresponded with abolitionist newspapers in America. He found the British "knew nothing of the republican Negro-hate prevalent in our glorious land."

Douglass's friends in England corresponded with an attorney and found out Capt. Thomas Auld would take £150 ($750) for Frederick Douglass's freedom. The papers releasing Douglass were signed on 13 November and 5 December 1846. He sailed to America in the spring of 1847 as a free man.

Douglass on the Abuse of Slave Women for Pleasure and Profit

Frederick Douglass

Frederick Douglass is the author of three autobiographies on his life as a slave and as an abolitionist and supporter of women's rights.

In the following viewpoint taken from Douglass's autobiography that followed Narrative of the Life of Frederick Douglass, *Douglass is more explicit in his descriptions of the suppression of family ties and the abuse of slave women, a subject that would have been shocking in Victorian society. In this piece, Douglass describes a haunting scene from his childhood, when he witnessed the sadistic beating of a slave woman who had angered her jealous master by meeting with a male slave.*

Could the reader have seen Captain Anthony gently leading me by the hand, as he sometimes did, patting me on the head, speaking to me in soft, caressing tones, and calling me his little Indian boy, he would have deemed him a kindhearted old man, and really almost fatherly to the slave boy. But the pleasant moods of a slaveholder are transient and fitful. They neither come often nor remain long. The temper of the old man was subject to special trials; but since these trials were never borne patiently, they added little to his natural stock of patience. Aside from his troubles with his slaves and those of Mr. Lloyd, he made the impression upon me of being an unhappy man. Even to my child's eye he wore a troubled and at times a haggard aspect. His strange movements excited my curiosity and awakened my compassion. He seldom walked alone

Frederick Douglass, *The Life and Times of Frederick Douglass*, Wordsworth Editions Limited, 1881, reprinted 1996. Reproduced by permission.

without muttering to himself, and he occasionally stormed about as if defying an army of invisible foes. Most of his leisure was spent in walking around, cursing and gesticulating as if possessed by a demon. He was evidently a wretched man, at war with his own soul and all the world around him. To be overheard by the children disturbed him very little. He made no more of our presence than that of the ducks and geese he met on the green. But when his gestures were most violent, ending with a threatening shake of the head and a sharp snap of his middle finger and thumb, I deemed it wise to keep at a safe distance from him.

Ignoring Overseer's Cruelty to Women

One of the first circumstances that opened my eyes to the cruelties and wickedness of slavery and its hardening influences upon my old master was his refusal to interpose his authority to protect and shield a young woman, a cousin of mine, who had been most cruelly abused and beaten by his overseer in Tuckahoe. This overseer, a Mr. Plummer, was, like most of his class, little less than a human brute, and, in addition to his general profligacy and repulsive coarseness, he was a miserable drunkard, a man not fit to have the management of a drove of mules. In one of his moments of drunken madness he committed the outrage which brought the young woman in question down to my old master's for protection. The poor girl, on her arrival at our house, presented a most pitiable appearance. She had left in haste and without preparation, and probably without the knowledge of Mr. Plummer. She had traveled twelve miles, barefooted, barenecked, and bareheaded. Her neck and shoulders were covered with scars, newly made, and, not content with marring her neck and shoulders with the cowhide, the cowardly wretch had dealt her a blow on the head with a hickory club, which cut a horrible gash, and left her face literally covered with blood. In this condition the poor young woman came down to implore protection at the hands of my old master. I expected to see him boil over with rage at the revolting deed, and to hear him fill the air with curses upon the brutal Plummer; but I was disappointed. He sternly told her in an angry tone, she deserved every bit of it, and if she did not go home instantly he would himself take the remaining skin from her neck and back. Thus the poor girl was compelled to return without redress, and perhaps to receive an additional flogging for daring to appeal to authority higher than that of the overseer.

The Results of a Complaint

I did not at that time understand the philosophy of this treatment of my cousin. I think I now understand it. This treatment was a part of the system, rather than a part of the man. To have encouraged appeals of this kind would have occasioned much loss of time and would have left the overseer powerless to enforce obedience. Nevertheless, when a slave had nerve enough to go straight to his master with a well-founded complaint against an overseer, though he might be repelled and have even that of which he at the time complained repeated, and though he might be beaten by his master, as well as by the overseer, for his temerity, the policy of complaining was, in the end, generally vindicated by the relaxed rigor of the overseer's treatment. The latter became more careful and less disposed to use the lash upon such slaves thereafter.

The overseer very naturally disliked to have the ear of the master disturbed by complaints, and, either for this reason or because of advice privately given him by his employer, he generally modified the rigor of his rule after complaints of this kind had been made against him. For some cause or other, the slaves, no matter how often they were repulsed by their masters, were ever disposed to regard them with less abhorrence than the overseer. And yet these masters would often go beyond their overseers in wanton cruelty. They wielded the lash

In his third autobiography, The Life and Times of Frederick Douglass, *the former slave turned author and abolitionist wrote in detail about his time as a slave and his escape to freedom.* © British Library/Robana via Getty Images.

without any sense of responsibility. They could cripple or kill without fear of consequences. I have seen my old master when in a tempest of wrath, and full of pride, hatred, jealousy and revenge, seem a very fiend.

The circumstances which I am about to narrate and which gave rise to this fearful tempest of passion, were not singular, but very common in our slaveholding community.

Sexual Motive Behind Abusive Beating

The reader will have noticed that among the names of slaves that of Esther is mentioned. This was the name of a young woman who possessed that which was ever a curse to the slave girl—namely, personal beauty. She was tall, light-colored, well formed, and made a fine appearance. Esther was courted by "Ned Roberts," the son of a favorite slave of Col. Lloyd, and who was as fine-looking a young man as Esther was a woman. Some slaveholders would have been glad to have promoted the marriage of two such persons, but for some reason Captain Anthony disapproved of their courtship. He strictly ordered her to quit the society of young Roberts, telling her that he would punish her severely if he ever found her again in his company. But it was impossible to keep this couple apart. Meet they would and meet they did. Had Mr. Anthony himself been a man of honor, his motives in this matter might have appeared more favorably. As it was, they appeared as abhorrent as they were contemptible. It was one of the damning characteristics of slavery that it robbed its victims of every earthly incentive to a holy life. The fear of God and the hope of heaven were sufficient to sustain many slave women amidst the snares and dangers of their strange lot, but they were ever at the mercy of the power, passion, and caprice of their owners. Slavery provided no means for the honorable perpetuation of the race. Yet, despite of this destitution, there were many men and women among the slaves who were true and faithful to each other through life.

But to the case in hand. Abhorred and circumvented as he was, Captain Anthony, having the power, was determined on revenge. I happened to see its shocking execution, and shall never forget the scene. It was early in the morning, when all was still, and before any of the family in the house or kitchen had risen. I was, in fact, awakened by the heart-rending shrieks and piteous cries of poor Esther. My sleeping-place was on the dirt floor of a little rough closet which opened into the kitchen, and through the cracks in its unplaned boards I could distinctly see and hear what was going on, without being seen. Esther's wrists were firmly tied, and the twisted rope was fastened to a strong iron staple in a heavy wooden beam above, near the fireplace. Here she stood on a bench, her arms tightly drawn above her head. Her back and shoulders were perfectly bare. Behind her stood old master, cowhide in hand, pursuing his barbarous work with all manner of harsh, coarse, and tantalizing epithets. He was cruelly deliberate, and protracted the torture as one who was delighted with the agony of his victim. Again and again he drew the hateful scourge through his hand, adjusting it with a view of dealing the most pain-giving blow his strength and skill could inflict. Poor Esther had never before been severely whipped. Her shoulders were plump and tender. Each blow, vigorously laid on, brought screams from her as well as blood. "Have mercy! Oh, mercy!" she cried. "I won't do so no more." But her piercing cries seemed only to increase his fury. The whole scene, with all its attendant circumstances, was revolting and shocking to the last degree, and when the motives for the brutal castigation are known, language has no power to convey a just sense of its dreadful criminality. After laying on I dare not say how many stripes, old master untied his suffering victim. When let down she could scarcely stand. From my heart I pitied her, and child as I was, and new to such scenes, the shock was tremendous. I was terrified, hushed, stunned, and bewildered. The scene here described was often repeated, for Edward and Esther continued to meet, notwithstanding all efforts to prevent their meeting.

Social Issues in Literature

CHAPTER 2

Slavery in
Narrative of the Life of Frederick Douglass

Preaching the Evils of Slavery

Robert G. O'Meally

Robert G. O'Meally is the Zora Neale Hurston Professor of English and Comparative Literature and the founder of the Center for Jazz Studies at Columbia University.

In the following viewpoint, O'Meally notes the influence of black sermon in Frederick Douglass's Narrative of the Life of Frederick Douglass. *Douglass's* Narrative *was his written sermon, intended to inform and convert his audience on the need to abolish slavery. Douglass refutes the slaveholders' biblical arguments that slaves are the justifiably damned sons of Ham by pointing out how many slaves have white fathers. He also argues that the slaves' so-called happy songs are actually the result of despair.*

The influences of the black sermon on black literature have been direct and constant. The Afro-American playwright, poet, fiction writer, and essayist have all drawn from the Afro-American sermon. Scenes in black literature occur in church; characters recollect particularly inspiring or oppressive sermons; a character is called upon to speak and falls into the cadences of the black sermon, using the familiar Old Testament black sermonic stories and images. . . .

What, then, is *sermonic* about Douglass' *Narrative [of the Life of Frederick Douglass]*? First of all, the introductory notes by William Lloyd Garrison and Wendell Phillips, both fiery orators and spearheads of the abolition movement, prepare the reader for a spiritual message. . . .

Robert G. O'Meally, "Frederick Douglass' 1845 Narrative. The Text Was Meant to Be Preached," *Afro-American Literature: The Reconstruction of Instruction.* Modern Language Association, 1979. pp. 192–211. Copyright © 1979 by Modern Language Association. All rights reserved. Reproduced by permission.

Introductions to *Narrative*

As if introducing the preacher of the hour, Garrison says that Douglass "excels in pathos, wit, comparison, imitation, strength of reasoning, and fluency of language." . . .

Wendell Phillips prepares the way for Douglass' "sermon." In his laudatory letter to the author, Phillips speaks of Southern white slave masters as infrequent "converts." Most often, the true freedom fighter detests slavery in his heart even "before he is ready to lay the first stone of his anti-slavery life." Phillips thanks Douglass especially for his testimony about slavery in parts of the country where slaves are supposedly treated most humanely. If things are so abominable in Maryland, says Phillips, think of slave life in "that Valley of the Shadow of Death, where the Mississippi sweeps along."

Testimony of the Evils of Slavery

Douglass' account of his life serves the ritual purpose announced in the prefatory notes: The ex-slave comes before his readers to try to save their souls. His purpose is conversion. In incident upon incident, he shows the slaveholder's vile corruption, his lust and cruelty, his appetite for unchecked power, his vulgarity and drunkenness, his cowardice, and his damning hypocrisy. Slavery, says Douglass, brings sin and death to the slaveholder. Come to the abolition movement, then, and be redeemed. Take, as Douglass has done, the abolitionist paper as a Bible and freedom for all men as your heaven. Addressed to whites, the *Narrative* is a sermon pitting the dismal hell of slavery against the bright heaven of freedom. . . .

Refuting Misconceptions of Slavery

In his effort to convert white slaveholders and to reassure white abolitionists, Douglass attempts to refute certain racist conceptions about blacks. He presents blacks as a heroic people suffering under the lash of slavery but struggling to stay alive to obtain freedom. To convince whites to aid slaves in their quest for freedom Douglass tackles the crude, prejudiced assumptions—which slavers say are upheld by Scripture—that blacks somehow *deserve* slavery, that they enjoy and feel protected under slavery. Of the notion that blacks are the cursed descendants of Ham [an individual who appears in the Old Testament], Douglass writes, "if the lineal descendants of Ham are alone to be scripturally enslaved, it is certain that slavery at the south must soon become unscriptural; for thousands are ushered into the world, annually, who, like myself, owe their existence to white fathers, and those fathers most frequently their own masters." Furthermore, if cursed, what of the unshakable conviction of the learned and eloquent Douglass that he is, in fact, chosen by God to help set black people free?

Slaves Learn to Suppress the Truth

What, then, of the assumption of the plantation novel and the minstrel show that blacks are contented with "their place" as slaves at the crushing bottom of the American social order? Douglass explains that a slave answers affirmatively to a stranger's question, "Do you have a kind master?" because the questioner may be a spy hired by the master. Or the slave on a very large plantation who complains about his master to a white stranger may later learn that the white stranger was, in fact, his master. One slave makes this error with Colonel Lloyd, and, in a few weeks, the complainer is told by his overseer that, for finding fault with his master, he is now being sold into Georgia. Thus, if a slave says his master is kind, it is because he has learned the maxim among his brethren "A still tongue makes a wise head." By suppressing the truth rather than taking the consequences of telling it foolishly, slaves "prove themselves a part of the human family." . . .

Songs Express Anguish, Not Joy

Do not the slaves' songs prove their contentedness and joy in bondage? "It is impossible," says Douglass, "to conceive of a greater mistake." Indeed, he says,

Ham is the son of Noah, from the Old Testament of the Bible, who had a curse put upon him for his sins. Many slaveholders used biblical arguments to condone slavery, suggesting that blacks were justifiably descendants of Ham who were meant to be servants to others. ©
UIG via Getty Images.

The songs of the slave represent the sorrows of his heart; and he is relieved by them, only as an aching heart is relieved by its tears. At least, such is my experience. I have often sung to drown my sorrow, but seldom to express my happiness. Crying for joy, and singing for joy, were alike uncommon to me while in the jaws of slavery.

Instead of expressing mirth, these songs Douglass heard as a slave "told a tale of woe which was then altogether beyond my feeble comprehension; they were tones loud, long, and deep; they breathed the prayer and complaint of souls boiling over with the bitterest anguish. Every tone was a testimony against slavery, and a prayer to God for deliverance from chains." These songs, Douglass recalls, gave him his "first glimmering conception of the dehumanizing character of slavery." In other words, these songs "prove" the black man's deep, complex humanity. Therefore, whites, come forth, implies Douglass, and join the fight to free these God's children! . . .

Effect of Slavery on Slaveholder

Like a sermon, too, Douglass' *Narrative* argues not only by stern reason but also with tales that may be termed *parables*. One of the most forceful of these parables, one threaded quite successfully into the *Narrative*, is the parable of poor Mrs. Auld. Residing in the border state of Maryland, in the relatively large city of Baltimore, Mrs. Auld, who has never owned a slave before she owns Frederick Douglass, is truly a good woman. Before her marriage, Mrs. Auld worked as a weaver, "dependent upon her own industry for a living." When eight-year-old Douglass is brought into the Auld household, Mrs. Auld is disposed to treat him with human respect and kindness. Indeed, "her face was made of heavenly smiles, and her voice was tranquil music." Douglass obviously presents this woman as a glowing model of Christian charity: "When I went there," he writes, "she was a pious, warm, and tender-hearted woman. There was no sorrow or suffering for which she had not a tear. She had bread for the hungry, clothes for the naked, and comfort for every mourner within her reach." Soon after Douglass arrives in her home, Mrs. Auld begins to do as she has done for her own son; she commences teaching Douglass the alphabet.

Before long, of course, this "kind heart" is blasted by the "fatal poison of irresponsible power." In Douglass' words, Mrs. Auld's "cheerful eye, under the influence of slavery, soon became red with rage; that voice, made all of sweet accord, changed to one of harsh and horrid discord; and that angelic face gave place to that of a demon." In response to her husband's warning that education "would *spoil* the best n----- in the world," she forbids Douglass' further instruction. In fact, she becomes at last "even more violent than her husband himself" in the application of this precept that slave education is a danger. Thus, even the mildest forms of slavery—in providential Baltimore—turn the most angelic face to that of a "harsh and horrid" devil. . . .

Sadism of Slaveholder

As noted, slavery turns the heart of "heavenly" Mrs. Auld to flinty stone. And Mr. Plummer, Douglass' first overseer, is "a miserable drunkard, a profane swearer" known to "cut and slash women's heads so horribly" that even the master becomes enraged. This enraged master, Captain Anthony, *himself* seems "to take great pleasure in whipping a slave." In a grueling scene, he whips [a female slave] until only the master's fatigue stops the gory spectacle. "The louder she screamed, the harder he whipped; and where the blood ran fastest, there he whipped longest." Mr. Severe would curse and groan as he whipped the slave women, seeming "to take pleasure in manifesting this fiendish barbarity." Colonel Lloyd renders especially vicious beatings to slaves assigned to the care of his horses. When a horse "did not move fast enough or hold high enough," the slaves were punished. "I have seen Colonel Lloyd make old Barney, a man between fifty and sixty years of age, uncover his bald head, kneel down upon the cold, damp ground, and receive upon his naked and toil-worn shoulders more than thirty lashes at the time." Other slave owners and overseers, both men and women, kill their slaves in cold blood. . . .

Douglass' *Narrative* is, in its way, a holy book—one full of marvels, demonstrating God's active participation in a vile and fallen world. The *Narrative* is a warning of the terror of God's fury. It is also an account of a black Moses' flight "from slavery to freedom." It is an invitation to join "the church" of abolition, a church that offers freedom not only to the slave and the sympathetic white Northerner but also to the most murderous and bloodthirsty Southern dealers in human flesh. Sinners, Douglass seems to chant, black sermon-style, you are in the hands of an angry God!

Countering the Slaveholders' Argument

Peter C. Meyers

Peter C. Meyers is professor of political science at the University of Wisconsin–Eau Claire and author of Our Only Star and Compass: Locke and the Struggle for Political Rationality.

In the following viewpoint, Meyers analyzes Frederick Douglass's ideas that the evil at the core of slavery was its treatment of human beings as animals through an immoral use of power, in practice ignoring that slaves were moral, intellectual, and responsible beings. Douglass sees slavery as an evil system from which evil individual behavior emerged. It is the antithesis of civilization. Slavery destroyed the natural social character of its victims by negating family and community, because the family had its own authority and could teach self-worth and independence. Meyers also notes that Douglass felt slavery's worst crimes were committed against children. This Douglass discovered in its true heinousness when he had children of his own.

[F]rederick] Douglass's insistence on slavery's unique, paradigmatic evil should not be passed over as a mere rhetorical intensifier. In the initial chapter of *[My] Bondage and [My] Freedom*, he disclosed the ruling principle of what he subsequently called slavery's "true philosophy." Its "grand aim ... always and everywhere, is to reduce man to a level with the brute." Despite their elaborate apologetics, slaveholders did not treat those they enslaved as mere children. Slavery's dehumanizing design was evident even in its structural definition: to subject any human beings to permanent, absolute, irre-

Peter C. Meyers, *Frederick Douglass: Race and the Rebirth of American Liberalism.* University Press of Kansas: 2008, pp 20–46. Copyright © 2008 by University Press of Kansas. All rights reserved. Reproduced by permission.

sponsible human power meant to treat them as if they were mere brutes. Douglass granted that slaveholders may not have commonly believed their slaves to be actually subhuman; their own statements and their equivocal practices suggested otherwise. They enacted no laws to govern their irrational livestock, he remarked in his Independence Day oration of 1852, whereas they did enact laws to govern slaves. "What is this," he asked, "but the acknowledgment that the slave is a moral, intellectual, and responsible being?" But slaveholders' equivocations did not mitigate their criminality. To the contrary, their deliberately brutal treatment of beings they knew to be human meant that a thoroughgoing mendacity and willfulness lay at the heart of slavery. . . .

The Roots of Evil Are in the System

Douglass's arguments for the intrinsic evil of slavery were only the beginning of his analysis. As he told a Baltimore audience in 1864, slavery, like liberty, was "logical"; from its defining relation flowed "an unceasing stream of most revolting cruelties." Because human nature is what it is, human beings in general will not freely accept absolute, perpetual subjection to their natural equals. Such subjection, violent in itself, can only be secured by violence both physical and spiritual. Slavery not only brutalized *formally*, by reclassifying some human beings as beneath the protection of laws, it also brutalized *effectively*, by endeavoring to transform them into brutes or domesticated animals, as the necessary means for perpetuating its treatment of them as such. Especially in this second sense, Douglass's insight into slavery's true philosophy accords with his mature analysis of slavery as a complex, logically organized *system* of injustice. As his partially sympathetic discussion of Aaron Anthony illustrates, slavery's effective evils were not, in the end, traceable finally to any gross vices in slaveholders' individual characters. Rather, its brutality was a systemic imperative.

In his carefully chosen illustrations of its brutalizing design at work, Douglass presented slavery as an extreme inversion of normal social and political life. Slavery was the epitome of barbarism, the antithesis of civilization. Civilized society fostered the conditions of human virtue and happiness, whereas slavery systematically destroyed them. To realize its paradoxical claim to human property, slavery required "the complete destruction of all that dignifies and ennobles human character." Asserting absolute power over body and soul, its physical cruelty was instrumental to its assault upon the qualities that elevate humankind above the lower animals. In Douglass's descriptions of the specific modes of this assault, we see more than devices for exciting shame and revulsion in his audiences; we gain a preliminary view of his understanding of the bases of human dignity. His account brings into view slavery's attempts to obliterate the human character of its primary victims as distinctively social, rational, spiritual, and moral beings. . . .

Slavery's Crimes Against Children

But despite the depth of slavery's outrages upon manhood and womanhood, its worst crimes were perpetrated upon children. In his public "Letter to My Old Master, Thomas Auld," written in 1848, Douglass declared, "A slaveholder never appears to me so completely an agent of hell, as when I think of and look upon my dear children. It is then that my feelings rise above my control." He indignantly contrasted his and his wife's authentic parenthood with the fraudulent paternalism of slaveholders. "These dear children are *ours*—not to work up into rice, sugar, and tobacco, but to watch over, regard, and protect, and to rear them up in the paths of wisdom and virtue." In *[My] Bondage and [My] Freedom* and *[The] Life and Times [of Frederick Douglass]*, young Frederick, relieved by his mother's angry rebuke of the Lloyds' cook, the cruel Aunt Katy, learned that he *belonged* to someone, by nature rather than by arbitrary force. . . .

Assault on Relationships

Slavery's assaults upon the distinctive rational, spiritual, and moral qualities of humankind, in Douglass's telling, accorded closely with its assault on human sociality. As Hugh Auld first had taught him, the acquisition of knowledge and especially knowledge of the Bible rendered one unfit for slavery. By reason or rational faith, one came to know the higher law that confirmed slavery's injustice. Mindful that nature or the Creator designed human beings for purposes nobler than enslavement, the thoughtful slave became increasingly miserable and potentially rebellious. To secure itself comfortably, slavery required the degradation of slaves' minds and souls. And the prohibition of slaves' literacy was the most obvious means to this end. Still further, Douglass observed that in important respects, slaves were deprived even of the power of speech—which, in conjunction with reason, was the most humanizing of mental powers. By various tactics of despotic surveillance, slaveholders aimed to engender a pervasive atmosphere of mistrust among slaves and thereby to prevent the exchanging of enlightening information and the formation of resistance schemes.

The Encouragement of Occasional Debauchery

In a more indirect mode, slavery's assault on rationality converged with its design to degrade slaves' moral character. Slavery ruled foremost by a constant excitement of the passion of fear. The field slave's daily motivation was "nothing, save the dread and terror of the slave-driver's lash," and for those slaves less regularly exposed to physical violence, there was the ever-present fear of being sold. In slave holidays, the rule of fear was momentarily replaced by the no less debasing rule of the lower appetites. Those holidays reinforced the masters' despotic power, both by providing a "safety valve" for the dissipation of slaves' anger and also by deepening the slaves' bru-

An image of Frederick Douglass with his grandson. Douglass felt slavery's worst crimes were committed against children, and he understood its true heinousness when he had children of his own. © UIG via Getty Images.

talization. On such occasions, all self-directed work and rational enjoyment were discouraged. Slaves were encouraged to plunge "into exhausting depths of drunkenness and dissipation," degrading at once their desire and their capacity for freedom. . . .

Slaveholders' Self-Justification

Douglass was confronted with the general objection by a slave-holding correspondent from Mississippi, one W.G. Kendall, whose letter he published in the *North Star* in 1850. After reading that journal for a year (having subscribed to assess the argument of an antislavery acquaintance), Kendall wrote to protest Douglass's *"indiscriminate abuse* of slaveholders." He complained that the former slave's account of slavery was "so highly colored, as not to be recognizable to the slave-holders." But Kendall offered no dogmatic defense of American slavery. He agreed with a Southern acquaintance that slavery was "a great curse" to whites and claimed that he would prefer to see it replaced immediately by a system of "voluntary slavery" akin to indentured servitude. He conceded, too, that the treatment of slaves needed improvement, but he maintained that their condition could be properly ameliorated without abolition. He commended to Douglass the same acquaintance's further opinion that even in its existing practice, slavery was a "great blessing to the black race." . . .

In response to Kendall, however, Douglass conceded not one inch. "Your fancied kindness, to what does it amount," he demanded angrily, "when set against the loss of liberty, the loss of progress . . . and the overwhelming degradation to which the slave is subjected. . . ? Perish all shows of kindness, when they are thought to conceal or to palliate the damning character of slavery." . . .

The imperative of self-justification required that slaveholders relocate slaves outside the class of rights-bearing beings. They could not do so by criminalizing them; the Lockean [referring to the teachings of English philosopher John Locke] justification of slavery had no application to American slavery. The only alternative was to ascribe to them natural inferiority. Douglass's moral psychology implies that the development of anti-black racism as a full-blown ideology resulted from the confrontation of the practice of slavery with the universalist natural rights principles to which America had dedicated it-self. But beyond establishing the premise of natural racial in-equality, slaveholders still had to convince themselves that their treatment of slaves was consistent with the obligations of civilized beings to inferior classes. As they brutalized their slaves in fact, they needed to believe that they were doing them no essential violence, even that they were civilizing them as far as the slaves' supposedly lower nature permitted. . . .

He assailed slavery as "the most stupendous of all lies"; its perpetrators were "as great liars, as they [were] great tyrants." Slaveholders first needed to be great tyrants over their own faculties, great liars to themselves as well as to others. To be a fully formed master, one with a good conscience, required a most impressive capacity for self-delusion.

Frederick Douglass and the Black Liberation Movement: The North Star of American Blacks

Wu Jin-Ping

Wu Jin-Ping is a professor of international relations at Jinan University in China where he specializes in American studies and international immigration.

In the following viewpoint, Jin-Ping argues that in writing of slavery in Narrative of the Life of Frederick Douglass, *Douglass focuses on the plight of slave women and their mixed-race children. Women were forced, as presumably his mother was, to have sex with white men. A woman's resistance to a white man who wanted sex with her resulted in savage beating, as is illustrated by the horrific scene the young Douglass witnessed as a child. Black women were not only sex objects but also slave-making machines because each child was worth money. Jin-Ping notes that Douglass emphasizes in* Narrative *that the ties between slave parents and children were deliberately severed so that the trade in slaves would not be complicated by natural affection. Douglass was not only separated from his mother, whom he scarcely knew, but from his grandmother, who raised him. His complicated relationship with these two women, with whom he had such emotional ties, likely accounted for his lifelong commitment to feminism as well as his dedication to end slavery.*

One of the greatest evils of slavery was to devastate women and families, as slaveholders often let their animal desires lead them to rape female slaves. No matter whether they were

Wu Jin-Ping, *Frederick Douglass and the Black Liberation Movement: The North Star of American Blacks.* Garland Publishing: 2000, pp. 9–10, 26–27, 28, 29. Copyright © 2000 by Taylor & Francis. All rights reserved. Reproduced by permission.

married or not, these women could be forced to have sexual intercourse with their owners, which sometimes resulted in pregnancy. In New Orleans, almost every young white man lived illegally with a black woman. Most of the cohabitations were the result of these rapes. If a black woman defended herself, she would be beaten savagely by the white man. Many women slaves carried the scars left when they resisted the advances of white men to their graves. Frederick Douglass once witnessed a terrible scene in which his owner beat his Aunt Esther savagely. Esther was a rather charming woman who had a slim body and a good-looking face. Her owner, Anthony, desired her very much, but she was in love with a fellow slave. Anthony, unable to stop their furtive meetings, became infuriated. He stripped her to her waist, hung her by her hands, and whipped her with a large cattle hide until blood dropped down her body while he cursed her "as a degrading prostitute."

The products of white rapes were many children of mixed blood, or mulattoes. Because the mulattoes were identified with their African American mothers, most were born into slavery. It appeared that the slaveholders were both their fathers and their owners. Under the slave system these slaveholder-fathers had no responsibility for their slave-children. Even if they wanted to care for these children, they would face the strong opposition of their infuriated wives and the whole society. It was also difficult for the slave-mothers to do much duty to their children. Frederick Douglass, for example, was brought up by his grandmother because he was separated from his mother, and he had little chance to see her. Douglass, moreover, did not even know who his father was. Someone told him that his father was Anthony, Douglass' owner, but Douglass was skeptical. It is almost certain that his father was a white man. And his case was not rare. In 1850, there were 246,000 mulattoes among 3,200,000 black slaves; in 1860, there were 411,000 mulattoes among 3,900,000 black slaves. The actual number was undoubtedly higher, because census workers only counted those who looked like mulattoes.

Slavery, however, treated women not only as sexual objects but also as machines for bearing babies. Frederick Douglass' grandmother, for instance, was once praised and rewarded by her owner for bearing so many children. When she gave birth to a baby, Anthony would reward her $2.40. Based on Anthony's account book of 1809, he apparently gave her $26.50 altogether for her eleven daughters. Anthony also gave her special permission: She would not work in the field but instead she would be a full-time childbearer. In the event that a slave woman did not bear children, an owner might force her to cohabitate with some healthy and strong slave men. John Brickell found this much out when visiting colonial North Carolina:

> It frequently happens, when these women have no children by the first husband, after being a year or two cohabiting together, the planters oblige them to take a second, third, fourth, fifth, or more Husbands or Bedfellows: a fruitful woman amongst them being very much valued by the planters, and a numerous Issue esteemed the Greatest Riches in this country.

Why did slaveholders do this? The answer is money. With the development of more and more large plantations, slaves were desperately needed. The slave trade became a way of making a fortune. Some slaveholders sold their surplus slaves to other slave dealers in the Deep South, and were rewarded handsomely. To ensure an ample source of slaves, these slaveholders forced their slave women to bear more and more children.

The Constitution of the Winthrop (Maine) Female Anti-Slavery Society pointed out that slavery was a system with the "intellects wasted, sentiments perverted, feelings outraged, and souls lost through the operation of a system which annuls the marriage tie, destroys all parental and filial obligation, denies the right of the mother to call her slumbering babe her own, produces every species of licentiousness and sets at naught the laws of God and nature." ...

The antislavery movement brought a ray of hope to those who lived under the slave system. Frederick Douglass was one of those who were led to escape from the shackles of slavery and free themselves under the guidance of that hope.

Even now there is an enigma to Frederick Douglass' life. When he was a little boy, he found that, unlike white children, most slaves did not know their birthdays. This haunted him throughout his life. He tried to find out when he was born and who his father was, but he failed. He could only guess that he was born in 1817, because "I heard from my master that I was about seventeen years old in 1835."

Later in 1845 he wrote that it "was a source of unhappiness to me even during childhood. The white children could tell their ages. I could not tell why I ought to be deprived of the same privilege." He concluded that "it is the wish of most masters within my knowledge to keep their slaves thus ignorant." Similarly, as his master deemed the question of a slave's birthday, like most inquiries by slaves, "improper ... impertinent, and evidence of a restless spirit," young Frederick Douglass certainly could not discover his birthday by asking his master. But in 1880, when he went back to Talbot County to meet his former master, Thomas Auld, Frederick Douglass did not forget to ask this question. Thomas Auld assured him that he was born in February 1818. However, Frederick Douglass did not believe it; he thought that he should be older. However, Dickson J. Preston believes that Frederick Douglass' birthday is a day in February 1818, rather than in February 1817. In the Anthony family archives, Preston found a written record compiled by Aaron Anthony and others that provides genealogical information on the slaves owned by the Anthony family. The notation on Douglass is in these words: "Frederick Augustus son of Harriott Feby 1818." Taken by itself, this record is persuasive but not conclusive. It is not in Aaron Anthony's handwriting. Apparently, it was inserted at a later day by an unknown person. This is the only written material concerning Frederick Douglass' birth date.

Toward the end of his life, Douglass still was not certain who his father was and when his birthday was. When he was young, he heard slaves saying in private that his old master, Aaron Anthony, was his real father, but he was not certain. In 1845, he wrote in his narrative: "My father is a white. All said so when my birth was discussed, and all hinted that my old master is my father. I didn't know whether it was true or not, for I could hardly know." From 1845, perhaps feeling embarrassed at having such a master-father, Frederick Douglass began to relate himself to Anthony less and less. In his second narrative, *My Bondage and My Freedom*, in 1855, in addition to the repetition of the above-mentioned story, he added that this was merely a story, and that he never believed it. On the contrary, Douglass assured his readers that Anthony was not his father. However, he did not deny the fact that his father was a white, and even said that he had Anglo-Saxon blood. In 1881, when he published his third narrative, *The Life and Times of Frederick Douglass*, he omitted all of the story about his father and Anthony, just saying that he knew nothing of his father. From his attitude toward his father and Anthony, one can see the pain being a mulatto caused him. Just as he recalled, the "penalty for having a white father" was very heavy. "A man who will enslave his own blood," he observed, "may not be safely relied on for magnanimity." The mulatto slave child represented "a standing accusation against him who is master and father to the child." For the master-father, that child signified a sin which he preferred to ignore. For the child, the results of this paternal rejection were painful. In Douglass' case, his non-relationship with his white father-master reinforced both his African American identity and his sense of racial ambivalence as a mulatto. It also heightened his

THE PARTING "Buy us too."

A painting showing a slave woman begging to be bought so that her family would not be separated. Ties between slave parents and children were deliberately severed so that the trade in slaves would not be complicated by family bonds. © Getty Images.

ambivalence toward whites in general and white paternal figures such as William Lloyd Garrison, his major abolitionist mentor, in particular.

Douglass' mother was one of Anthony's women slaves, Harriet Bailey. She was a daughter of an African American couple. The history of the Bailey family could be traced to June 1764, when Eastern Shore became one part of Maryland. They had lived there for more than half a century, and Douglass was the fifth generation of that family. By the end of the eighteenth century, the slaves in the Eastern Shore had lived in family units since that time, which was to say that a typical slaveholder held only a man slave, a woman slave, and their children, sometimes including several generations. This was why the Bailey family could survive as a family for so long a time. And for that reason, the Bailey family was very proud. They were rooted deeply in the Eastern Shore, and their culture and values were of America, not of Africa. Thus, it is easy to understand why Douglass strongly opposed the removal of African Americans from the United States when he grew up. . . .

However, Douglass knew little about his mother, because he was separated from her when he was very young. It was the custom for a slave child to be separated from his mother when he was weaned from the breast, or less than a year old. Douglass was brought up by his grandmother, while Harriet was hired to a slaveholder twelve miles away. Douglass could only remember that she came to see him several times at night, because she could only visit after she had finished her field work and walked for twelve miles. She then had to go back to work before daybreak, or she would suffer from the whips. Thus every time she came, Douglass always fell asleep quickly in her arms, and when he woke up, she had gone. On an unknown day, she died on a farm in Tuckahoe. Douglass did not know of her death until long after she died. When he heard the news, he did not feel sorrowful; it was as if he had just heard the news of a stranger's death. For him, their long separation dulled the trauma of her death. Not until he grew up did he understand her love, which slavery had tempered. Douglass recalled that "the pains she took, and the toil she endured, to see me, tell me that a true mother's heart was hers, and that slavery had difficulty in paralyzing it with unmotherly indifference."

Slavery, Douglass often emphasized, had deprived him as a child of a traditional familial environment. He declared that "there is not, beneath the sky, an enemy to filial affection so destructive as slavery. It had made my brothers and sisters strangers to me; it converted the mother that had bore me, into a myth; it shrouded my father in mystery, and left me without an intelligible beginning in the world." . . .

As mentioned earlier, Douglass was brought up by his grandmother, Betsey Bailey. As he recalled later, her gentle hand and kind deportment had engaged his infantile understanding and her love stood in place of his mother's. . . .

According to custom, Douglass was sent to his master's house when he was six years old. Aaron Anthony had three farms and thirty slaves, which were managed by his overseers, while he himself was the general overseer of the Lloyd Plantation, the biggest plantation on the Eastern Shore. The Anthony family lived on the Lloyd Plantation, and Frederick Douglass was taken there in the summer of 1824. The shock of separation from his beloved grandmother proved severe. He did not understand why she left him alone. He recalled: "I had never been deceived before and something of resentment mingled with my grief at parting with my grandmother." He stressed subsequently that while the incident might seem trivial to others, he could not "withhold a circumstance which at that time affected me so deeply, and which I still remember so vividly. Besides, this was my first introduction to the realities of the slave system."

The trauma of Frederick's separation from his grand-mother was pivotal to his comprehension of his enslavement, his increasing desire to be free, and his eventual decision to run to freedom. His maturation enhanced, yet eventually eased, the burden of both his emotional loss and the perception of his grandmother's related powerlessness and degradation. Similarly, he eventually gained a deeper awareness of both the deeply buried, though, inescapable, emotional loss which his mother's death entailed for him and her own related powerlessness and degradation. Frederick's commitment to feminism, therefore, might have represented in part his life-long attempt to grapple with his stunted maternal tie. It might also have represented to a degree his attempts to grapple with the relationship between sexism and racism. The deep-seated emotional influence of the separations from his mother and grandmother thus probably contributed to his dedication to racial and feminist liberation specifically and social reform generally.

Slavery Robs Its Victims of Identity

Henry Louis Gates Jr.

Henry Louis Gates Jr. is a professor at Harvard University and director of the W.E.B. Du Bois Institute for African and African American Research. Besides his many authored and edited books, Gates has written and produced Finding Your Roots, *a PBS series.*

In the following viewpoint, Gates emphasizes the importance of knowing concrete information about one's past. Frederick Douglass was missing important information about his beginnings, such as his birth date and the identity of his father, and consequently he felt a loss of personal identity. Gates points out that Douglass's yearning to know who his father was presented even toward the end of his life; this was shown by an unproductive visit he made to someone he thought might have information. Douglass guessed something about his age by consulting the seasons and animal births after his master's death, when he was first sent to Baltimore. Douglass dealt with this gap in his life by creating his own identity as writer and speaker, with the representation of a public self.

By the end of 1894, Frederick Douglass had begun to prepare for his death. Unbowed and energetic even to the last, Douglass had, however, apparently reconciled himself to "live and rejoice," as he put it in 1881, to occupy with dignity and gravity that peculiar role conferred upon him by friend and foe, black countryman and white, contemporary and disciple alike: He was "The Representative Colored Man of the

Henry Louis Gates Jr., *Figures in Black: Words, Signs, and the "Racial" Self.* Oxford: Oxford University Press, 1987, pp. 98–124. Copyright © 1987 by Oxford University Press. All rights reserved. Reproduced by permission.

United States." Despite the unassailable respect he commanded throughout the country, one bit of common knowledge had never been Douglass's to possess, and, as Peter [F.] Walker movingly recounts it, the final entry in his *Diary* suggests that it haunted him to death.

Still Searching for Identity

On a March 1894 evening, just less than a year before he died, Frederick Douglass left his home at Anacostia and boarded a train for the brief ride from Washington to Baltimore. At Baltimore, Douglass went directly to the home of a physician, Dr. Thomas Edward Sears. After a carefully calculated but leisurely conversation, during which Douglass put to Dr. Sears a series of specifically formulated questions, Douglass returned by train to Washington and then by coach to Anacostia Heights. Early the next morning, he went to his study, took out his *Diary*, and wrote as that day's entry an account of his trip to Baltimore. This was to be the final entry in Douglass's *Diary*. In the final months remaining to him, no other event moved Douglass sufficiently to record another entry in his little *Diary*. . . . Sears, a descendant of Douglass's old master, would be the last contact Douglass was to have with the family that had once owned him. More important, Sears had some information about his slave past that Douglass wanted, and all his self-conscious life Douglass had pursued passionately all concrete information about his lost, or hidden, past. . . .

No Documentation of Self

A sense of self as we have defined it in the West since the Enlightenment turns in part upon written records. Most fundamentally, we mark a human being's existence by his or her birth and death dates, engraved in granite on every tombstone. Our idea of the self, it is fair to argue, is as inextricably interwoven with our ideas of time as it is with uses of language. In antebellum America, it was the deprivation of time in the life of the slave that first signaled his or her status as a piece of property. Slavery's time was delineated by memory and memory alone. One's sense of one's existence, therefore, depended upon memory. It was memory, above all else, that gave a shape to being itself. What a brilliant substructure of the system of slavery! . . .

Standing Outside of Time

We recall that although Douglass knows where he was born (in Tuckahoe, near Hillsborough, about twelve miles from Easton, in Talbot County, Maryland), his date of birth is not for him to know. A "slave" was he or she who, most literally, stood outside of time. To the end of his life, the mystery of his birth remained for Douglass what he called "a serious trouble" and helps us to understand why a man in his seventy-sixth year took the trouble to mount one final attempt to obtain facts about his existence. The skeletal facts of Douglass's journal entry, as Peter [F.] Walker cites it, suggest the pathos of the unconsummated quest:

> I called yesterday while in Baltimore . . . upon Dr. Thomas Edward Sears, a grandson of Thomas and Lucretia Auld and learned the following facts:
>
> Capt. Thomas Auld, was born 1795
>
> Amanda Auld, his daughter was born Jan. 28, 1826
>
> Thomas, son of Hugh and Sophia Auld was born Jan. 1824
>
> Capt. Aaron Anthony, Died Nov. 14, 1823.

"The Death of Aaron Anthony," Douglass concluded, "makes me fix the year in which I was sent to live with Mr. Hugh Auld in Baltimore, as 1825." At last, Frederick Douglass possessed a major "fact." From his master's death, Douglass could extrapolate the date he was sent to Baltimore as a boy, that key signpost on his personal road to freedom. Perhaps emboldened by the specificity of Aaron Anthony's date of death, Douglass concluded this curious *Diary* entry by being even more specific about when in 1825 he had come to Baltimore, even if, like the slaves, he once more dated the passage of time by the movements of the animals and the seasons: "I know it must have been in the summer of that year that I went to live in Baltimore because the spring lambs were big enough to be sent to market, and I helped to drive a flock of them from Smith's Dock to Fells Point on the day I landed in Baltimore." With this memory of lambs in summer, Frederick Douglass's *Diary* ends, as did his lifelong quest to locate facts that could bolster the limitations of memory. Beyond 1825 and Baltimore, Douglass was not ever able to verify his own memory. . . .

Defining Himself and His Mission

To Douglass the autobiographer, his life was the vehicle for a social program. Accordingly, he served as editor and censor of even the smallest bits of data about his life until he had rendered them in language as part of the public self that he spent forty-seven years retouching. If Frederick Douglass was the nineteenth century's Representative Man, it was primarily because of his mastery of the literary uses of spoken and written language, a usage he diligently reworked and refined, splendidly. Frederick Douglass was no slave to the English language. Douglass himself seems to have given a priority to the spoken word over the written word. As he wrote in 1849, "Speech! Speech! The live, calm, grave, clear, pointed, warm, sweet, melodious, and powerful human voice is [the] chosen instrumentality" of social reform. While writing served its purpose, some matters were of such urgency that the spoken word was demanded. "Humanity, justice and liberty," wrote Douglass, "demand the service of the living human voice." . . .

Long after the issues for which he struggled so ardently have become primarily the concern of the historian, Frederick

Douglass will continue to be read and reread. And surely this must be the literary critic's final judgment of Frederick Douglass: that he was Representative Man because he was Rhetorical Man, black master of the verbal arts. Douglass is our clearest example of the will to power as the will to write. The act of writing for the slave constituted the act of creating a public, historical self, not only the self of the individual author but also the self, as it were, of the race.

Douglass Battles Oppression to Gain Literacy and Power

Philip S. Foner

Philip S. Foner (d. 1994) was a professor at Lincoln University and author of 110 published works, including several volumes on black workers and Thomas Paine.

Foner points out that Frederick Douglass came to realize at a young age that literacy was the key to knowing one's rights and other people's wrongs against slaves, and was, therefore, the key to power and liberation. The young Douglass sensed this after his brief schooling by Sophia Auld before her husband intervened. From that moment on, Douglass secretly grasped that power for himself. Douglass used his newly acquired literacy to teach others through speeches he wrote and delivered to further the abolitionist movement.

For seven years Douglass worked for Hugh Auld, first as a household servant and later as an unskilled laborer in his shipyard. During the period he experienced comforts such as he had never known before. Yet he was seldom allowed to forget that he was a slave. Hearing his new mistress, Sophia Auld, read the Bible, a burning desire to learn to read consumed him. In response to his plea, his mistress taught him the alphabet and how to spell words of three or four letters. But the lessons ended the moment her husband learned of the boy's progress. In Douglass' presence, Hugh Auld forbade further instruction, shouting that "learning would *spoil* the best n----- in the world." Once a slave knew how to read there would be no keeping him!

Philip S. Foner, *The Life and Writings of Frederick Douglass: Early Years, 1817–1849*, pp. 15–27. Copyright © International Publishers. All rights reserved. Reproduced by permission.

Learning Despite Obstacles

These words only inspired the boy with a greater determination to learn. His former teacher was now the chief obstacle; as if to atone for her error, she kept constant vigilance over him, snatching any book or newspaper she saw in his hand, and making sure he could obtain no reading matter. But by various ingenious devices Douglass continued his education. He turned to school boys in the streets in out-of-the-way places where he could not be seen, and converted them into teachers. Out of his pocket would come the leaves of books he had raked "from the mud and filth of the gutter," a copy of his Webster's spelling book, and a slice of bread to pay for the lessons. While his tutors munched the bread, he talked to them about slavery. "Have not I as good a right to be free as you have?" he would ask the urchins. He was comforted by their sympathy and by their confidence that something would yet happen to make him free.

With the first fifty cents he earned by blacking boots he bought the popular school book *The Columbian Orator*. This book deepened his hatred of slavery, and as he read and memorized the speeches of Chatham, Sheridan, and Fox in behalf of human rights, he began to understand his position. He was a victim of oppression, and if these great men were right, it was wrong that he or any man should be doomed to slavery. As he walked about the streets repeating to himself the words of Sheridan and Chatham, he kept asking himself: "Why am I a slave? Why are some people slaves, and others masters? Was there ever a time when this was not so? How did the relation commence?" He found no satisfactory answer to these questions, but when he heard his master and his friends denounce the abolitionists, he resolved to discover who and what they were. Finally, in the columns of the *Baltimore American* he found a report that a vast number of petitions had been submitted to Congress, praying for the abolition of the internal slave trade. From that day, probably sometime in February, 1833, "there was hope."

The thought of escaping from slavery frequently occurred to him. Two Irishmen whom he had met on the wharf advised him to run away to the North where he would be free. But he hesitated. He was still too young, and he wished to learn to write so that he himself could fill out the necessary pass.

While working in the shipyards he mastered the essentials of writing. During the slack periods he would copy the letters that made up the names of the ships; then using the streets as his school, his playmates as teachers, and the fences as his copybooks and blackboards, he learned to write. In later life in responding to a request for his autograph, he said: "Though my penmanship is not too fine it will do pretty well for one who learned to write on a board fence." ...

Teaching Forbidden

When Douglass began to teach a Sunday school class for colored children, Master Auld decided that he had better take steps to provide his young slave with proper conditioning. Consequently, on the following Sunday, men armed with sticks and stones invaded the school, disrupted the class, and warned the teacher "to watch out." Douglass seemed determined to be another Nat Turner [an African American slave who led a rebellion in Virginia], said Master Auld, and if he did not mend his ways he would most certainly "get as many balls into him" as had the Negro slave rebel of 1831. Actually, Turner was hanged, but despite the inaccuracy, the warning indicated that trouble lay ahead.

Competition for Jobs

For the next two years, from the summer of 1836 to the summer of 1838, Douglass worked in the Baltimore shipyards, first as an apprentice, then as a skilled caulker. During the first eight months of apprenticeship he came to know, through bitter experience, "the conflict of slavery with the interests of the white mechanics and laborers of the South." Forced to compete with slaves, the white workers found it impossible to get decent wages. Consequently they sought to keep slaves out of the trades, and demanded the ousting of all Negro artisans, free as well as slave. When such a drive got under way at the shipyards of William Gardner on Fell's Point where Douglass was apprenticed, he became the victim of the campaign. Douglass was attacked many times. At one time, he fought his attackers so violently that it required four white apprentices, armed with bricks and heavy hand spikes, to finally lay him low. He was long to remember with bitterness how fifty white mechanics stood about during this brutal attack, some crying, "kill him—kill him—kill the d—d n-----, knock his brains out—he struck a white person." Much later in his life he came to understand that the Southern white worker was almost as much the victim of the slave system as was the Negro. . . .

Learning from Free Blacks

In the evenings, after a day's work in the shipyard, Douglass extended his education. He met free Negroes who were well versed in literature, geography, and arithmetic, and he sought to learn from them. As a slave he was not able to join any of the forty benevolent institutions established by the free Negroes of Baltimore, but he was permitted to become a member of the East Baltimore Improvement Society as a special concession. Here he took a prominent part in debates and here, too, he met Anna Murray, who afterward became his wife. . . .

Beginning of His Oratory

The day-to-day task of eking out an existence for a growing family did not afford Douglass many opportunities to satisfy his longing for education. But he applied the same ingenuity that had stood him in good stead as a slave. "Hard work, night and day, over a furnace hot enough to keep metal run-

William Lloyd Garrison was an abolitionist and newspaper publisher in Massachusetts whose writings and speeches inspired Frederick Douglass to join the abolitionist movement. © Corbis/AP Images.

ning like water was more favorable to action than thought," he wrote later, "yet here I often nailed a newspaper to the post near my bellows and read while I was performing the up and down motion of the heavy beam by which the bellows were inflated and discharged."

Soon after they had settled down in their new home, Douglass began to make himself a part of the Negro community of New Bedford. Having been class leader and choir member of the Sharp Street Methodist Church in Baltimore, he sought to renew his religious contacts. He joined a local Methodist church, but remained there only a short time. He discovered that Negroes were second-class communicants, sitting in a special section of the church. In disgust he walked out of the church, never to return. He tried other churches in New Bedford with the same result, and finally joined a small sect of his own people, the Zion Methodists, where he soon became a leading member of the congregation and a local preacher.

Before he had left Baltimore, Douglass had already heard of the abolitionists and of their work to end slavery. He had received help from them en route to New Bedford, but actually he knew very little of their activities. Four months after he had come to New England there came into his hands a copy of William Lloyd Garrison's the *Liberator*. So deeply was he moved by the paper that despite his poverty he became a regular subscriber. Every week he read the journal avidly, studying its principles and philosophy. "The paper became my meat and my drink," he wrote six years later. "My soul was set all on fire. Its sympathy for my brethren in bonds—its scathing denunciations of slaveholders—its faithful exposures of slavery—and its powerful attacks upon the upholders of the institution—sent a thrill of joy through my soul, such as I had never felt before!"

Douglass was not satisfied to sit at home and thrill to the paper. He began to attend the abolitionist meetings held by the Negro people of New Bedford. The first printed reference to Frederick Douglass appeared in the *Liberator* of March 29, 1839. It reported an anti-colonization meeting of the Negro citizens of New Bedford at the Christian Church on March 12, at which Douglass was one of the speakers in favor of resolutions condemning slavery, commending Garrison "as deserving of our support and confidence," and denouncing the African colonization movement in the following terms:

"That we are *American citizens*, born with natural, inherent and just rights; and that the inordinate and intolerable scheme of the American Colonization Society shall never entice or drive *us* from our native soil."

Douglass became more and more involved in the abolitionist activities of the New Bedford Negroes. Every fortnight he attended a social meeting at the home of John Baily to discuss antislavery principles and events. A white abolitionist who attended these sessions observed that in the discussions "the colored people acquire the habit of thinking and speaking; a circumstance which may, in a great measure, account for the self-possession of their manners, and the propriety and fluency of their language." Among these New Bedford abolitionists Douglass was gradually assuming a position of leadership. On June 30, 1841, he was chairman at a meeting called to censure the Maryland Colonization Society for "threatening to remove the free colored people out of that state by coercion." The Negroes urged their brethren in Maryland to resist intimidation and condemned an attack on David Ruggles who had been roughly handled for combating segregation on the steamboat operating between New Bedford and Nantucket.

On August 9, 1841, Douglass attended the annual meeting of the Bristol Anti-Slavery Society, held in New Bedford. Here in old Liberty Hall, a large, dilapidated building, with doors off their hinges, windows broken by stones thrown to break up abolition proceedings, Douglass first heard William Lloyd Garrison. It was a red-letter day in the life of the young Negro, barely twenty-four years of age and but three years removed from slavery, because on that day, he saw in the editor of the *Liberator* the mission for his own life. "It may have been due to my having been a slave," he wrote toward the end of his life, "and my intense hatred of slavery, but no face and form ever impressed me with such sentiments as did those of William Lloyd Garrison." Douglass himself entered into the discussion and made a distinct impression upon the abolitionist leader who reported to his paper that at the meeting were "several talented young men from New Bedford, one of them formerly a slave whose addresses were listened to by large and attentive audiences with deep interest." . . .

Proving His Manhood

The next morning, August 12, at the convention in Athenaeum Hall, Douglass was called upon to speak by William C. Coffin, a New Bedford abolitionist. Douglass, trembling and ill at ease, came forward to the platform and spoke with deep sincerity of his own life as a slave. Greatly stirred, Garrison followed with an exciting address using Douglass' remarks as his text. He asked the audience, "Have we been listening to a thing, a piece of property, or to a man?" "A man! A man!" came from five hundred voices. Then he asked if they would ever allow Douglass to be carried back to slavery and received a thunderous "No!" in reply. "Will you succor and protect him as a brother man—a resident of the old Bay State?" was the next question. "Yes!" shouted the audience with such vehemence that "the walls and roof of the Athenaeum seemed to shudder."

That evening Douglass spoke again, and, as in the morning, the group was moved by his eloquence. In his report of the convention, the *Anti-Slavery Standard* correspondent devoted special attention to the Negro delegate from New Bedford:

"One, recently from the house of bondage, spoke with great power. Flinty hearts were pierced, and cold ones melted by his eloquence. Our best pleaders for the slave held their breath for fear of interrupting him. Mr. Garrison said his speech would have done honor to [American founding father] Patrick Henry. It seemed almost miraculous how he had been prepared to tell his story with so much power. In the evening, which was to be the last meeting, he was again called forward, and listened to by a multitude with mingled emotions of admiration, pity and honor. . . .

"Then Garrison arose, and burst forth into a more eloquent strain than I had ever heard before. He eulogized, as he deserved, the fugitive who had just spoken and anathematized the system that could crush to the earth such men."

Before the convention adjourned, John A. Collins, general agent of the Massachusetts Anti-Slavery Society, urged Douglass to become an active lecturer for the organization. Douglass was reluctant to accept, doubting his own ability, but finally agreed to work for the society for three months. He was to travel with Stephen S. Foster, and, in addition to lecturing, was to get subscriptions for the *Liberator* and the *Anti-Slavery Standard*. His salary was to be four hundred and fifty dollars a year.

Douglass returned to New Bedford convinced that his usefulness as an abolitionist agent would not last beyond the three-month period. Events were rapidly to show how seriously he had underrated himself, and to prove that this was but the launching of a great career.

Religious Belief and Slavery

Scott C. Williamson

Scott C. Williamson is a professor of theological ethics at Louisville Seminary, where he specializes in African American studies.

In the following viewpoint, Williamson examines the ways Frederick Douglass's relationship with religion changed throughout his life. As a child, Douglass began to question what he had been taught about a good God, his creator. His natural independence of mind also caused him to doubt that in God's plan, some were meant to be masters and some, like him, to be slaves, whose duty it was to submit to their masters without question. Douglass came to a belief in God as a father and protector after listening to a Methodist preacher. He also believed that God's purpose for him was not to submit but to fight against the enslavement of all peoples. Williamson notes that this was a radical rejection of the moral teachings of the white pro-slavery clergy. Slaveholders, unlike slaves, have freedom of choice, and the highest evidence of a slaver's acceptance of God was to free his slaves.

> **Why am I a slave? Why are some people slaves, and others masters? Was there ever a time when this was not so? How did the relation commence?**

These sorts of questions figure among the earliest ones [Frederick] Douglass entertained about his slave status while a young boy on the Lloyd plantation. The questions came about as a result of the brutal floggings of his Aunt Esther and of a cousin from Tuckahoe. Witnessing some of the "gross features" of slavery prompted Douglass to attempts at self-examination.

Scott C. Williamson, "The Slave Episode," *The Narrative Life: The Moral and Religious Thought of Frederick Douglass*. Mercer University Press, 2002, pp. 31–64. Copyright © 2002 by Mercer University Press. All rights reserved. Reproduced by permission.

Questions About God and Slavery

His attempts led him to questions about the character of God. Douglass, along with the other children, was sent to Isaac Copper—Uncle Isaac—to learn the Lord's Prayer. Douglass did not discuss the efficacy of his encounter with Uncle Isaac. Rather, he reflected on his inquiries to the other children about God: "I learned from these inquiries, that 'God, up in the sky,' made everybody; and that he made white people to be masters and mistresses, and black people to be slaves. This did not satisfy me, nor lessen my interest in the subject."

Far from lessening his interest, the responses elicited from other children only slightly older than Douglass introduced a paradox begging resolution. He was told that God was good but this answer did not help to explain the cruel treatment Aunt Esther endured. Douglass instinctively drew a large distinction between notions of goodness and Esther's punishment. "It was not good to let old master cut the flesh off Esther, and make her cry so." At the time, Douglass concluded that God may have made white men to be slaveholders, but He did not make them to be bad slaveholders. Douglass thought bad slaveholders would surely be punished for their iniquities. His notions of God and of goodness did not fit with the cruelties of slavery.

Slavery Made by Man, Not God

Douglass continued to question the relation between God and the "peculiar institution." He wrote in his 1855 narrative: "I was not very long in finding out the true solution of the matter. It was not color, but crime, not God, but man, that afforded the true explanation of the existence of slavery; nor was I long in finding out another important truth, viz: what man can make, man can unmake."

The exact source of these conclusions is unclear. In this context the excerpt establishes the point at which Douglass came to an understanding of slavery as an evil perpetuated by whites, and not as a good ordained by God.

This view of slavery did not develop in a vacuum. . . . Douglass clearly endorsed a perspective that countered the approbation and "official answer" of slaveholders. Douglass's interaction with fellow slaves on the Eastern Shore helped him to appraise the morality of slavery. Given his social location, what he saw of slavery, and what he knew of freedom, Douglass was persuaded at an early age that slavery was a criminal institution of oppression. . . .

The Need for God

Douglass learned from his master that education was a means of resistance to slavery, but he was less certain about religion's role in that regard. He believed that slavery was not of divine origin. God remained obscure to Douglass, hidden in platitudes and prayers. While in Baltimore, Douglass had his first experience of a personal encounter with God.

Beyond formal religious doctrine, Douglass came to need God, "as a father and protector." This longing for God was intensified by the preaching of a white Methodist minister named Hanson:

> I cannot say that I had a very distinct notion of what was required of me; but one thing I knew very well—I was wretched, and had no means of making myself otherwise. Moreover, I knew that I could pray for light. . . . After this, I saw the world in a new light. I seemed to live in a new world, surrounded by new objects, and to be animated by new hopes and desires. I loved all mankind—slaveholders not excepted; though I abhorred slavery more than ever. My great concern was, now, to have the world converted. . . .

Freedom Ordained by God

As his hatred of slaveholders was changed by religion, so too his hatred of slavery was changed by his religious beliefs. Though no less adamant about emancipation, Douglass wrote that the zeal of his hatred for slavery became enlisted in a broader campaign for conversion. In other words, he accepted religious reasons for freedom beyond the personal reasons he entertained previously. Convinced that freedom was ordained by God, and that sinfulness obtained universally, Douglass came to believe that not only his enslavement but slavery as an institution needed to end. The upshot is that Douglass began to distinguish between a private ethic grounded in an "unofficial answer" to the morality of slavery and a public or social ethic. Douglass came to see that there was more at stake than his own freedom. Conversion confirmed for him that God intended freedom for all people; education provided him with a new and formal way to make the case. . . .

Slave Holding Unforgivable

Interestingly, Douglass's sense of being deceived and cheated by slaveholders was not alleviated by his religious convictions. That was one sin Douglass seemed unable to forgive or forget. The hypocrisy of slaveholders who performed evil in the name of good always aroused Douglass's ardor.

Hanson brought Douglass to an understanding of the wretchedness of all people, and to the power of prayer. It was a black man named Lawson, however, who became Douglass's spiritual mentor. Though he was scarcely able to read, he taught Douglass the gospel. . . .

God's Purpose for Douglass

Lawson's assurances that Douglass would be useful in the world were welcomed by the younger man. Lawson inspired Douglass, and in his words Douglass found an incentive to continue hoping for deliverance from bondage. With this hope again enlivened, Douglass recommitted himself to his quest for knowledge. The notion that God had a purpose for him other than to be a slave enabled Douglass to enlist religion along with education in his quest for freedom. Having already learned how to read, he focused on learning how to write. This activity consumed his remaining time in Baltimore. . . .

Morality in Society

Douglass, like other slaves, was not bound by the moral teachings of the slaveholders' church, choosing instead to think for himself on the matter while retaining his religious convictions. His moral thought in this instance is unique. . . .

Douglass referred to a "slave society," yet maintained that this society did not share in the morality of slaveholders. This leads one to the conclusion that slaves on a plantation lived within a discrete moral system. Next, however, he claimed that slaves had no moral responsibility. If slaves had no moral responsibility, to what extent did they comprise a society? What then is the moral basis of their community? What were its defining beliefs? If, on the other hand, Douglass intended to argue that slaves had no moral responsibility vis-à-vis slaveholders, what did that mean for the slave community itself? Was it a discrete social community, competent to think morally, or did it acquiesce to the dominant slaveholding morality by its own moral inability? I believe that Douglass intended something akin to this correction: Slavery disallowed moral comity between slaves and slaveholders, and therefore disallowed the moral accountability of slaves to their masters. In other words, the biblical commandment "Thou shall not steal" established a moral duty for slaveholders and for slaves *within their respective communities*, but did not impose a moral obligation upon slaves to their masters.

Slaveholders, however, were caught in a moral conundrum. Unlike their human chattel, slaveholders enjoyed freedom of choice. Freedom, in turn, established an obligation to moral responsibility. By prosecuting slaves for crimes such as theft, slaveholders revealed twisted logic and dysfunctional moral judgment. They demanded slaves to be morally responsible *to whites*, though coercion and violence were normative practices. Conversely, slaveholders acknowledged no such responsibility to slaves, though they enjoyed freedom of choice. Hypocrisy, duplicity, and immunity were the cardinal compass points of slaveholding power.

Slaves resided in a culture and a community that reflected their understanding of the good. This culture was not removed from the larger slaveholding culture, but on the contrary rose in response to the abuses of the larger culture. Similarly, the morality of slave culture reflected the teachings of Christianity, but it screened out the hypocrisy of slaveholding Christianity and made Christian tenets applicable to the lives of slaves.

Slaveholders and
Their Religion

Donald B. Gibson

Among the books authored or edited by Donald B. Gibson, Professor Emeritus at Rutgers University, are From Heaven He Came and Sought Her *and* Black and White: Stories of American Life.

In the following viewpoint, Gibson reflects on Frederick Douglass's frank portraits of cruel, immoral so-called religious slaveholders in Narrative of the Life of Frederick Douglass *that led him to clarify his religious views in the appendix to the work. Gibson claims Douglass's intention was to make a distinction between the slaveholders' false Christianity and true Christianity, although Gibson believes that Douglass's distinction is illogical. Still Douglass realized that in attacking the entire Christian church, in both the North and South of a country that tolerated slavery, he was positing a radical thesis. At the time of the writing of* Narrative, *the Quakers were the only Christian denomination that took a decided stand against slavery.*

Frederick Douglas certainly knew that there existed the possibility—even the likelihood—that his narrative could be read as an expression of doubt and apostasy. For that reason he added an appendix, a contrary one; ordinarily, appendixes are taken out for reasons of health—not put in. Frederick Douglass puts his in for the sake of sanitizing the implications of the *Narrative [of the Life of Frederick Douglass]*. . . .

Ideal Christianity vs. American Religion

Though Douglass certainly seems committed to Christian belief during his narrative, there is some reason to believe that

Donald B. Gibson, "Faith, Doubt, and Apostasy. Evidence of Things Unseen in Frederick Douglass's Narrative," *Frederick Douglass: New Literary and Historical Essays.* Cambridge University Press: 1990, pp. 84–95. Copyright © 1990 Cambridge University Press. All rights reserved. Reproduced by permission of Cambridge University Press.

he felt a more than passing hostility to Christianity. The distinction he makes in the appendix between American Christianity and ideal Christianity, a distinction made by many others in antislavery polemic, is logically nice, so it seems to me, but in fact impossible. When Christ says to Peter, "Thou art Peter, and upon this rock I establish my church," the trope intends to connect an ideal church, a church whose existence is outside of time and history, with a material world. The similar distinction that Douglass and others make is based on the assumption that those logical categories have real existence. But if we agree with William James that "feeling is the deeper source of religion, and that philosophic and theological formulas are secondary products, like translations of a text into another tongue," then we might infer that Douglass's love for Christianity and his abhorrence of it both live in the same house, the former, perhaps, on a lower level than the latter.

The virulence of Douglass's characterization of American Christianity in the appendix barely masks a deep-rooted anger and hostility, anger not only at the men who make up the church (I use the word "men" advisedly; there is not a single reference in the appendix to Christians as women), but also at the vehicle that makes possible the hypocrisy of which he speaks. . . .

Douglass's Radical Doctrine

Douglass says, in effect, that whatever appears in the *Narrative* that could be read as anti-Christian is justified because of the church's participation in and support of slavery. He feels that he must defend himself because he knows that the distinction he and other abolitionists make between the "American" church and the "true" church is not a distinction acceptable to most, especially in a country where one might have been exiled or worse for saying the same thing less than 200 years before. He knows that he is expounding a radical doctrine, one that most Christians will not accept with equanimity. He is, after all, attacking the church and all its denominations, both North and South. "The religion of the South . . . is by communion and fellowship the religion of the North" (*Narrative*, 157).

By 1845, when Douglass was writing the *Narrative*, not one of the major denominations other than the Quakers held a strong antislavery position. Earlier, this was not the case. In the eighteenth and early nineteenth centuries, antislavery sentiment was strong among Baptists, Methodists, and, of course, Quakers. The course of the relations between the church and slavery was essentially similar among the various religious sects. . . .

The More Religious a Slave Owner, the More Cruel

Douglass also has a vitriolic anger toward Christians and organized Christianity because his own experience and knowledge led him to believe that the more religious a slave owner, the more mean, vicious, and cruel he is likely to be: "Were I to be again reduced to the chains of slavery, next to the enslavement, I should regard being the slave of a religious master the greatest calamity that could befall me. For of all slaveholders with whom I have ever met, religious slaveholders are the worst" (*Narrative*, 117). Douglass tells us that they are the worst because the license given them by a slaveholding society is buttressed by a religion that actively supports a system ultimately, it was claimed, sanctioned by God. After his conversion to Methodism in 1832, Thomas Auld, Douglass's owner at the time, was, indeed, not more humane and kind: "If it had any effect on his character, it made him more cruel and hateful in all his ways; for I believe him to have been a much worse man after his conversion than before. Prior to his conversion, he relied upon his own depravity to shield and sustain him in his savage barbarity; but after his conversion, he found religious sanction and support for his slaveholding cruelty" (*Narrative*, 97). Douglass particularizes his observation by describing Auld's bloody lashing of Henny, a young lame slave girl, whom he has tied up for that purpose. While he lashes her with a cow-skin whip, he recites one of the two Bible verses used almost exclusively as texts for sermons preached to slaves. "He that knoweth his master's will, and doeth it not, shall be beaten with many stripes" (Luke 12:47). The other was "Servants, be obedient to them that are your masters according to the flesh, with fear and trembling, in singleness of your heart, as unto Christ" (Ephesians 6:5). . . .

Separating God from Slavery

To preserve religious belief, it was necessary for him to distance God from slavery. On two occasions in the *Narrative* he raises the question of God's existence, the theodicy question that must have arisen in the mind of every slave exposed to Christianity: If there is a God, why am I a slave? and Is there a God? Douglass asks the question once as he stands on the Maryland shore, looking out onto Chesapeake Bay, lamenting his condition: "Is there any God?" (*Narrative*, 106). Another time he raises the question as he remembers his beloved, yet still enslaved, companions who attended his Sabbath school in Maryland before his escape: "Does a righteous God govern the universe?" (*Narrative*, 14).

Very often it was most difficult for slaves to preserve religious faith, either because of the incredible contradictions between the two institutions or because of the conditions of slavery. . . .

In order to deal with these vexing conundrums, Douglass finds himself, given his temperament, in the position of either denying God's existence or explaining the existence of slavery in such a way as to disallow God's participation in it. Early on, as he begins his reading of *The Columbian Orator*, he decides that slavery is the responsibility of men (*Narrative*, 84). His experience with [Edward] Covey convinces him of several

Frederick Douglass traveled throughout the United States, and later England, telling of his experiences as a slave and speaking out against the practice of slavery. © ASSOCIATED PRESS.

things. It teaches him, first, that he delivered *himself* out of the arms of slavery and, second, that God is not responsible for the evil that men do. He also learns that no root, such as that offered him by Sandy, his fellow slave, will be efficacious in protecting him from abuse. He becomes one of our early pragmatists (qualifiedly so) in that he comes to believe in a very practical Christianity, a worldview that places politics ahead of religion insofar as the managing of the affairs of life is concerned.

A Practical Approach

Such a practical bent ran throughout his thought during the course of his career. His early speeches found him saying that "he had offered many prayers for freedom, but he did not get it until he prayed with his legs." During a period of intense debate about whether slaves should be sent the Bible, he said on more than one occasion: "Give them freedom first, and they will find the Bible for themselves." At another time he responded scathingly that it would be "infinitely better to send them a pocket compass and a pistol!"

The expression of such sentiments led to Douglass's reputation in some quarters, before and after the Civil War, as an infidel. It was in part his reaction to such charges that lay behind the composition of the appendix, where his declaration that "I love the pure, peaceable, and impartial Christianity of Christ" is a clear and direct denial of infidelity (*Narrative*, 153). His belief, expressed in the appendix, that Christians would deny fellowship to a "*sheep*-stealer," yet harbor a "*man*-stealer, and brand me with being an infidel" for pointing it out, refers directly to the charge and implies that it was widespread indeed (156). . . .

There is a measure of realism in Douglass's thinking that separates it from that of most people of his time and, at the same moment, makes him a man of his time. The hard, objective view he takes of religion, a view that allows him to consider it unsentimentally and dispassionately, caused him to be known as an unbeliever in a climate totally intolerant of anything suggesting doubt or unbelief. Such an appellation, however, he shared with the advanced thinkers of the nineteenth century, many of whom were beginning to see religion in its social and historical dimensions. Douglass saw it in its political dimension as well, as an institution inseparably bound to human affairs. The appendix is one of Douglass's many efforts to see the church objectively, to drive a wedge between faith in God and support of the Christian church, which, as the appendix conceives it, was the most "peculiar institution" of all.

Douglass's *Narrative* as a Work for Abolition

Houston A. Baker Jr.

A distinguished professor at Vanderbilt University, Houston A. Baker Jr. specializes in the African American experience. His books include The Journey Back *and* Blues, Ideology and Afro-American Literature.

In the following viewpoint, Baker explains how Frederick Douglass used different literary techniques to stir emotions in his white readers. Douglass uses animal imagery (like beasts of burden) to reinforce his view of the dehumanization of slavery, wishing that he could be a thoughtless beast to be relieved of his mental anguish. Narrative of the Life of Frederick Douglass *also makes use of folk themes for converting readers to the cause of abolition. Indeed his is the most sophisticated of the slave narratives and is an example of his working through the existing system to accomplish his purpose. At the same time,* Narrative's *sophistication led many white readers to doubt that a former slave could have written it.*

One can scarcely treat the agrarian settings and characters in [Frederick] Douglass's *Narrative [of the Life of Frederick Douglass]* without some discussion of the animal metaphors that appear in most of the chapters of the *Narrative*.

Slave as Beast of Burden

We have already noted the quip about the horse who does not know his age; and Douglass uses a similar figure to describe his joy when given the chance to go to Baltimore: "It was al-

Houston A. Baker Jr., *Long Black Song: Essays in Black American Literature and Culture*, pp. 75–80. © 1972 by the Rector and Visitors of the University of Virginia. Reprinted by permission of the University of Virginia Press.

most a sufficient motive, not only to make me take off what would be called by pig-drovers the mange, but the skin itself." Speaking of the anguish that resulted from a grasp of his situation, Douglass comments: "In moments of agony, I envied my fellow-slaves for their stupidity. I have often wished myself a beast. I preferred the condition of the meanest reptile." These images, of course, serve to reinforce Douglass's descriptions of the "soul-killing" effects of slavery; in a word, they make the effects of the three-fifths clause immediate. Slaves, like horses and other wild animals, were "broken." . . .

Survival Tactics

Douglass's work is a chronicle of the "soul-killing" effect slavery had on both master and the slave. Time and again in the *Narrative* men's hopes for a better life are crushed: Humans are whipped and slaughtered like animals; men and women are changed into maniacal and sadistic creatures by power; the strength of mind and body is destroyed by an avaricious and degrading system. Captain Auld, Douglass and his fellow slaves, Mrs. Hugh Auld, Mr. Covey, Anthony Auld—practically every character we encounter in the *Narrative* is rendered less human by the effects of slavery. Douglass's work, however, does not simply describe the degradation occasioned by slavery; it also illustrates how a sense of community, a spirit of revolt and resistance, and a mastery of disguise and deportment—black survival values which we encountered in the folk tradition—assist in the development and ultimate escape of the person who is willing to employ them. We are confronted in the *Narrative* with a record of the early development of one individual, a *Bildungsroman*, which records the growth to manhood of a small slave boy whom we first see in a tow-linen shirt enjoying a relatively work-free life. Then we see a boy at twelve years of age playing the trickster in order to acquire the rudiments of education. . . .

At sixteen the boy adopts the code of the bad-man hero and wrestles a fierce slave breaker into submission, vowing after the struggle that "the white man who expected to succeed in whipping, must also succeed in killing me." The nineteen-year-old *man*, with his fellow slaves, makes an abortive attempt for freedom, and the twenty-year-old man finally gains his liberty. . . . Douglass does not tell us so in the *Narrative*, but he made his escape to the North by wearing a sailor's uniform and travelling as a free man.

We must admit that at times the author grows maudlin (in describing the plight of his grandmother, for example), and at times he is clearly too rhetorical (the soliloquy by the bay). For the most part, however, he is a candid, witty and thorough narrator, able to play the diverse stops of the human condition with consummate skill. It seems appropriate, therefore, to classify the *Narrative* as a consciously literary work, and one of the first order. The black folk background manifests itself in the values that make survival possible in a brutal system, as well as in individual incidents, such as that in which Sandy Jenkins gives Douglass a root for his protection. . . .

The Importance of Escape

Although the connection of Douglass's work with the black American folk tradition is clear, his obvious concern for the craft of writing places the *Narrative* in the realm of sophisticated literary autobiography. More specifically, Douglass's work is a spiritual autobiography akin to the writings of such noted white American authors as Cotton Mather, Benjamin Franklin, and Henry Adams. The narrator wishes to set before the reader not only his fully realized spiritual self, but also the hallowed values that made possible such a self. The *Narrative*, however, can be distinguished from the works of white American spiritual autobiographers because its essential goal is physical freedom. The narrator is not seeking to become one among the divine elect, nor is he attempting to forge a pri-

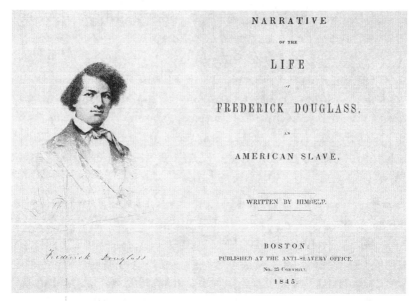

Title page and engraved portrait from Narrative of the Life of Frederick Douglass, *Douglass's first book detailing his experiences as a slave.* © Bettmann/CORBIS.

vate, moralizing self as a foil to an intensely practical and political age that stressed the virtues of the public man. He seeks to move, by any means necessary, from a cruel physical bondage to freedom. . . .

Public Suspicion of *Narrative's* Literary Sophistication

Although an orator himself, Frederick Douglass . . . was not interested in rendering the intonation and diction of oratory into written form. . . . Douglass effectively applies sophisticated literary techniques—irony, wit, caricature, understatement, humor; he never lacks the right word or the proper anecdote to emphasize his point; and he relies upon masterful and convincing literary presentation rather than fiery rhetoric. In fact, it is the passages in which he lapses into oratory that detract from the overall effect of his work. . . . *Narrative of the Life of Frederick Douglass* manifests the values of the Garrisonian [referring to William Lloyd Garrison] abolitionist reformers who were in favor of moral suasion and opposed to any interaction (especially that of a political character) with slaveholders. . . .

Douglass's is one of the most finished of many slave narratives, which generally were written for abolitionist purposes and principally for white readership. The incentive for this work was provided by reports that many whites in the audiences Douglass addressed under the auspices of the Massachusetts Anti-Slavery Society could not believe such polished speeches came from a man who had been a slave. . . .

Douglass intended to convince his white readers that he had suffered the dire effects of slavery, presumably hoping that in their moral outrage they would first acknowledge his remarkable achievement and then go forth to protest the abuses of slavery in America. The prime motivating force for his work and his Garrisonian stance help to explain his restrained posture and sophisticated style.

In some ways these same factors distinguish Douglass's work from the poorer slave narratives. In his attempts to persuade and convince, the author was forced to go beyond the format that was later to become standard for the slave chronicle. We are confronted with a host of fully rounded characters in the *Narrative*; we have a number of finely drawn scenes presented one after the other; and while we sense the irony, we also sense the genuine feeling of sincerity in the work. Only a few American narratives have such characteristics.

Social Issues
in Literature

CHAPTER 3

Contemporary
Perspectives on Slavery
in the United States

Agricultural Slaves

Erin C. Heil

Erin C. Heil is in the Department of Sociology and Criminal Justice Studies at Southern Illinois University. She is the author of Powerless Resistance.

In the tomato fields near Immokalee, Florida, workers were virtual slaves until investigators like Erin C. Heil uncovered the situation. In the following viewpoint, Heil records how the workers received no pay except occasionally in produce, performed forced labor in high temperatures without breaks, were subjected to physical violence, and were not allowed to leave. She notes they were under both physical and psychological constraints. These conditions were hidden away, as the fields were far from the nearest town of Immokalee, where the workers were trucked occasionally.

It is dusk, as the sun is beginning to set on a Friday evening in Immokalee [a small town in Florida]. The workers have just stepped off of the work buses, each worker carrying a watermelon in hand.

Paid in Produce

The officer sitting with me scoffs to himself: "Looks like they got paid in produce today." I turn to him with a look of surprise, to which he only responds with a shrug of his shoulders. It is quite possible that these workers were paid with produce rather than cash. They have just worked over ten hours under the sun of a blistering 85-degree day with little to no break, and all they have to show for their work is one wa-

Erin C. Heil. Selected passages from pp. 25–52 of *Sex Slaves and Serfs: The Dynamics of Human Trafficking in a Small Florida Town*. Copyright © 2012 by FirstForum Press, a division of Lynne Rienner Publishers, Inc. Used with permission by the publisher.

termelon. No worker bothers to complain, for that would only result in termination from work, financial losses, and/or physical and psychological violence. Therefore, each worker hangs his head as he steps off the bus, cradling a watermelon in his arms. . . .

Hidden Slavery in Immokalee

Visiting the town of Immokalee, it is difficult to fathom that for eight months of the year, this is predominantly an agricultural migrant community. The town is small, and there are virtually no fields to harvest. There are factories at the edge of town that finalize the production of produce, and there is a pinhooking market selling the leftovers of the daily harvest, but there are no visible fields within the city limits. This is because the fields are located miles outside of town on back roads that are difficult to navigate for drivers who do not regularly travel them. If one were able to stumble upon a tomato field, there would seem to be nothing more than a botanical wall or fence, which obstructs any view of the workers. Entry is available to a select few, as hired security block the entrance.

Even if a glimpse may be caught of the workers, the first view of slavery is so overwhelming that the workers become one, a single mass of generalizable characteristics. From this distant perspective, the workers, wearing baseball caps to offer some protection from the sun, appear to be the same height. Skin is blistered and browned; hands are calloused and permanently blackened by the soil. Heads hang low as tomatoes are picked and buckets are hoisted and carried on shoulders. The workers become one, but each individual is unique in his own experience. However, as an outsider, I am unable to move beyond this quick glimpse of the enslaved farmworkers, for the farmers and the field bosses assure that this forced labor will remain hidden one way or another.

Because of the obstacles of entry and observation of the migrant workers in the field, I employed alternative methods to develop a clear image of who is working in the fields. I observed the early evening drop-off of workers by the labor buses, and I analyzed the demographic information revealed in arrest reports, including occupation, age, and country of origin. With this methodology, I was able to develop a typology of the field-workers based on age, gender, and country of origin. . . .

The Character of Slave Labor

"80 percent of the migrants in Florida are illegal immigrants and thus especially vulnerable to abuse," including low wages, intolerable conditions, and virtually no legal protection. According to [John] Bowe:

> The average migrant has a life expectancy of just forty-nine years. Twenty thousand farm workers require medical treatment for acute pesticide poisoning each year; at least that many more cases go unreported. . . . An estimated 80 percent [of Florida farm workers] have no work papers, and . . . their average yearly pay [is] an estimated $6,574.

The work is literally backbreaking, as laborers must carry and unload approximately two tons of tomatoes a day just to elevate their earnings to a minimum-wage payday. In general, the workday begins at five in the morning; potential workers wait over an hour for a contractor to choose who will work in the fields that day. The farmworkers cannot pick any tomatoes until the morning dew has been burned off by the sun, so they must wait until approximately 9:00 am before they can begin the picking process. This waiting period is unpaid. Once they are able to begin picking the tomatoes, the workers must engage in the constant choreography of bending down to pick the tomato and then placing the tomato in a basket. Once the basket is full, the workers hoist it onto their shoulders and

Migrant workers toil on a tomato farm in New Jersey. Such workers can be found on farms throughout the United States, and some are forced to work in slave-like conditions. © James Leynse/Corbis.

must run the tomatoes to the truck without spilling or damaging the product. This dance is performed for hours on end with no time for a break. . . .

Punishments for Trying to Escape

Two . . . social restraints that maintain the system of slavery are physical and psychological. According to one detective I spoke with, the workers are almost completely imprisoned by psychological chains. "Traffickers create an environment of fear meant to control their victims." There are no gates to keep the workers from escaping, but the workers are aware of the penalty if they escape and are caught. The detective continued:

> If a worker escapes and is found, he will be brought back [to the farm] by the slavers. At the farm, the other workers must stop what they are doing and watch as the man who tried to escape is beaten by three or four [handlers]. You

have to remember that the worker is small and weak. The men beating him are sometimes three times his size.

The beatings are meant to be imprinted into the minds of the other workers and are a lesson to anyone else who tries to escape. For some, the stories passed down regarding the punishment for escape are enough to keep the workers from leaving before paying off their debt. Just the knowledge that this is a potential result, whether real or a story told through the seasons, creates enough psychological stress to rule out a chance of escape.

Other than the beatings (or threat of a beating), the workers face immense fear for their families in their country of origin. Both victim advocates and legal professionals report that the workers will not speak out against their handlers because of the direct ties to their families. Traffickers have either directly stated or insinuated to the farmworkers that if they try to turn to the local police for assistance, their families will be murdered. This is usually not an empty threat because of the relationship between many of the workers and the traffickers. . . . In most trafficking cases, the traffickers have developed a relationship with the family members remaining in the country of origin. This relationship ensures an element of control over the workers, as they realize that their families are under surveillance and are in danger if the worker crosses the trafficker. . . .

Slavery Throughout the United States

Agricultural slavery is widespread throughout United States. In fact, the Coalition of Immokalee Workers [CIW] estimates that at any one time, approximately 5 percent of U.S. farmworkers are subjected to forced labor. However, due to the invisibility of agricultural slaves, the number is arguably much higher than the CIW estimates. . . .

Immokalee is not unique in its being a hub for agricultural slavery, for this form of forced labor is evident in all corners of the United States. From the tomato pickers in Florida to the strawberry harvesters in California, no agricultural community is completely immune from the possibility that the migrant laborers, especially those who are undocumented, are forced to work in slave-like conditions. Agricultural slaves have been identified in small apple orchards in Illinois, as well as Christmas tree fields in the Northeast. As long as there is a demand for cheap labor, as well as a vulnerable undocumented migrating population, agricultural slavery will persist in the United States. . . .

Beyond the immigration status of identified slaves, the general experiences of those trapped in slavery are similar throughout the country. [According to the group Anti-Slavery International,] in the majority of identified cases in the United States:

> an element of debt bondage is involved. Traffickers promise to take workers on credit to well-paid jobs where the debt incurred for transport can be paid off quickly. In some instances, workers arrive at the place of work already thousands of dollars in debt. Subsequently they are forced to pay off their debts in conditions to which they did not agree, working in the fields for 12–14 hours a day, seven days a week. Deductions are made from their wages for transport, accommodation, food, work equipment, and supposed tax and Social Security payments. Weekly wages are sporadic and in many instances workers are left with no pay.

In addition:

> Workers are coerced in a number of ways and the violent treatment of victims can be extremely traumatic. Enslaved workers are taken to labor camps where they face brutality and a near-total loss of control over their lives. As many as 12–16 pickers may be housed in one cramped, run-down trailer, kept under constant surveillance by employers using a variety of methods, including armed guards. Some endure a constant barrage of verbal abuse along with threats of vio-

lence and death to themselves and their families back home. In the most severe cases, employers use public beatings, pistol-whippings, and shootings to make an example of those trying to escape. . . .

Beyond the development of farmworker advocacy organizations, after reading this [viewpoint], readers are now more aware of the general indicators among the migrant class trapped in agricultural slavery. Lack of identification, the inability to leave a job, constant surveillance by field bosses, and the inability to speak for oneself are strong indicators associated with victims of agricultural slavery and human trafficking. Readers may also be more aware of the fresh produce available in their own community, yet they may still be unaware of where the produce is harvested. Perhaps upon deeper investigation, readers may identify agricultural slavery in fields on the outskirts of their own town. . . . Entering Immokalee for the first time, an outsider would not be aware of the slavery associated with the tomato industry, for the evidence of forced labor is miles outside of the center of town. Attentiveness to these indicators will assist more and more members of the general public in identifying victims of agricultural slavery and reporting suspicions to the properly trained authorities. This [viewpoint] serves not only to identify agricultural slavery in Immokalee, but also to illuminate the reality of trafficking for purposes of forced labor throughout the United States. With the general similarities of victims of trafficking and agricultural slavery, this [viewpoint] provides the reader with the basic indicators and warnings that slavery is not an issue of the past, or of another country, but rather is evident in farming communities throughout the United States.

Labor Exploitation and Human Trafficking of Mexican Nationals to the Gulf Coast

Stephanie Hepburn

Stephanie Hepburn is a lawyer, an independent journalist, and the author of Human Trafficking Around the World: Hidden in Plain Sight.

In the following viewpoint, Hepburn describes how the devastation caused by Hurricanes Katrina and Rita offered opportunities for unscrupulous contractors to make money from slave labor. There was a pressing need for construction workers to rebuild structures that had been decimated by the storms, and, at the same time, little enforcement of worker protection laws. Job safety and health standards were suspended for the laborers who often worked twelve-hour days, seven days a week. To control workers, contractors confiscated their legal documents, explains Hepburn. The workers were kept confined, guarded in labor camps, and promised less than a minimum wage, which was confiscated to pay off their recruitment fees.

In the wake of Hurricanes Katrina and Rita, buildings and lives were simultaneously destroyed. There was an immediate need for low-cost labor during a time of lawlessness when worker-protection regulations were suspended and enforcement of existing laws was almost nonexistent, creating an ideal scenario for labor exploitation and human trafficking.

Conditions of Slavery

To envisage post-Katrina New Orleans and the conditions its workers faced, simply imagine a city of tents erected in what was formerly a popular golf course in New Orleans City Park.

Stephanie Hepburn, "Aftermath of Hurricanes Katrina and Rita: Labor Exploitation and Human Trafficking on Mexican Nationals to the Gulf Coast," as in *Borderline Slavery: Mexico, United States, and the Human Trade*, eds. Susan Tiano and Moira Murphy-Aguilar. Ashgate Publishing Company: 2012. Reproduced by permission.

Inside those tents were mostly day laborers living in subhuman conditions, without running water or bathroom facilities. Laborers often worked twelve-hour days, seven days a week. Most were paid a fraction of what they had been promised or were not paid at all.

In one publicized case, over 500 workers were allegedly forced to live in guarded labor camps in Orange, Texas, and Pascagoula, Mississippi. According to the complaint against their employer, Signal International, LLC, the victims were each charged about $20,000 in fees for recruitment, visas, and travel. Upon arrival in the United States, the men were placed in the guarded labor camps, their travel documents were confiscated and their movements were significantly restricted. The workers were housed in groups of two dozen in single modular structures. The aisles between their bunk beds were so narrow that the workers had to turn sideways to walk through them. At one point, five of the workers were illegally detained and locked in a room monitored by armed guards.

Another case involves persons brought into the United States ostensibly to engage in agricultural tasks in North Carolina, but who were instead forced to perform demolition work and live in dilapidated New Orleans buildings. Kept in the buildings by an armed guard and with no money for food, the victims at one point had to trap pigeons in order to eat.

In both of these cases, the workers appear to have been victims not merely of labor exploitation, but of human trafficking. To date, at least 3,750 persons have been identified as potential victims of human trafficking into the Gulf Coast region in the post-Katrina period. Many of them traveled to the region voluntarily but were forced into debt peonage and indentured servitude after they arrived. . . .

Forced Labor and Debt Bondage

Even though human trafficking is directly prohibited under the federal Victims of Trafficking and Violence Protection Act of 2000 (TVPA), the lack of monitoring of construction sites as well as loosened labor laws in the post-hurricane Gulf Coast resulted in a scenario ripe for forced labor and debt bondage.

On September 5, 2005, the Occupational Safety and Health Administration of the Department of Labor (DOL) temporarily suspended the enforcement of job safety and health standards in hurricane-impacted counties and parishes in Florida, Alabama, Mississippi and Louisiana. On that same day, a memorandum by the Employment Standards Administration of the DOL issued a three-month suspension of Affirmative Action requirements with respect to federal contracts related to Hurricane Katrina relief efforts.

Presumably to accommodate survivors who had lost documentation and to jump-start the rebuilding process, on September 6, 2005, the Department of Homeland Security (DHS) suspended, for a period of 45 days, the requirement that employers confirm the eligibility and identity of their employees. Two days later, former president George W. Bush decreed a two-month suspension of the Davis-Bacon Act, which guarantees construction workers the prevailing local wage when paid with federal money.

These suspensions resulted in a lack of enforcement, not the least of which was a significant decrease in DOL investigations in New Orleans. According to Ohio Representative Dennis Kucinich, the number of DOL investigations in New Orleans dropped from 70 in 2004 to 44 in 2006. The result was a 37 percent decrease in investigations at a time when, according to Kucinich and others, the city needed more, not less, labor law enforcement. With the suspensions and lack of enforcement of labor laws throughout the region, it became commonplace for migrant workers in the post-hurricane Gulf Coast to face toxic work conditions with inept or nonexistent protective gear, twelve-hour workdays for seven days per week, and nonpayment of wages and/or overtime.

One Worker's Testimony

Hector, a New Orleans migrant worker, aptly described his post-Katrina experience in the Southern Poverty Law Center report (2006), *Broken Levees, Broken Promises: New Orleans' Migrant Workers in Their Own Words*. He faced nonpayment and inhumane working conditions as well as long-term medical side effects:

> "The work we were doing in the schools was horrible," Hector told interviewers. "The hurricanes had left the schools full of mud—three or four feet of mud. All sorts of filth was in the mud. There were horrible smells, and we found snakes, frogs and a lot more."

> ". . . At five in the morning, we were already standing and waiting for the company bus to pick us up. At seven or eight at night, we would still be at work because the bus hadn't come yet to take us back to the hotel. We would be suffering from the cold and hunger because we only ate once in the evenings. Imagine working a whole day on only water. Since we weren't being paid for our work, we didn't have any money to feed ourselves. We ate only in the evenings when the hotel helped us."

Since working in the schools, Hector hasn't been well. In the mornings when he showers, he finds dried blood in his nose. "I feel like something has damaged me. I had to endure all this just to work in order to earn a living," said Hector.

> "I believe that the contractors don't have a heart to be touched. Poor people come here to work, to better the city, to do the cleanup and to help out. These contractors, all they want is to hoard money. They don't care whether you eat or not. They just want to get the money and run away with it as many companies have done. Many companies have contracted people at a certain wage, but when the time comes to pay them, they just decide they don't want to pay it anymore. . . ."

Enslavement Through Confiscation of Passports

In the aftermath of Hurricane Katrina, roughly 130 Mexican guest workers were hired by a company called Louisiana Labor, LLC. Matt Redd, owner of the real estate company Redd Properties, LLC, allegedly started Louisiana Labor, LLC, in order to bring in H-2B [a visa for temporary employment in the United States] laborers from Mexico and rent them out to local businesses.

> "Matt . . . went to Mexico," said [Saket] Soni. "He, himself, became a recruiter. He went to Mexico, recruited workers, promised them that for $400 they would be transported to Louisiana in airplanes—charged them $400 for airfare. When he received the $400, he then packed the Mexican workers into vans like sardines and confiscated their passports and essentially trafficked them across the border to Louisiana."

According to Soni, once in Louisiana the workers were crammed into apartments in buildings owned by Redd Properties. Redd then leased the workers out to work for various businesses such as restaurants, casinos, car washes, and a fabric shop. A former employee of Louisiana Labor, LLC, [Nestor] Vallero states that he was promised a stable job, dignified housing, suitable working conditions, and fair wages.

> "When we got here, however—well, even before we crossed the border the lies became evident," said Vallero. "They stole our passports. They only gave them to us to present to the immigration officials, but then they took them away again.
>
> Then we got to the apartments and, there, we were crammed into rooms. They had said there would only be four people to an apartment, and they said that we'd have our own bathroom and everything. But the living conditions turned out to be deplorable."

The workers were told that upon arrival they would be working in construction but instead were placed in a variety of menial jobs with wages far below what they had been promised. When workers brought up the issue of wages, Redd and his associates allegedly told them that they could go home if they didn't like the wages. When passports were addressed, the workers were allegedly told that they would only receive their passports if they were going home. The workers were also allegedly charged exorbitant housing costs that placed them further in debt.

> "After all of this, we were just forced to take whatever job they were offering us, because we didn't have any money to go home or do anything else," said Vallero. "But that wasn't all. They started to discount the cost of our housing from our wage[s] . . . we had to pay $1,200 a month for housing. Out of a $300 check that we received for two weeks' work, they would take/discount almost $200 off that check. So, they're really, you know, raking in the profits with our work. It's really just a money-making scheme, this whole guest workers program."

This story is echoed by Fernando Rivera, another alleged victim of Redd. According to Rivera, Redd would simply lease out the workers for his own financial gain. When Rivera asked for his passport to be returned to him, Redd refused and threatened to call immigration. "Matt Redd would sell us to the highest bidder," Rivera told the *Nation*. "The money passed through his hands and afterward there was never very much left. It was hell there, but there was nothing else to do but bear it."

Threats and Cruelty

A classic case of trafficking is that of 42 to 118 guest workers from Mexico who were allegedly brought to perform labor in Amite, Louisiana, by Charles Relan, the owner of Bimbo's Best Produce. Relan allegedly confiscated the workers' passports and temporary H-2A visas; threatened them with unlawful eviction, arrest and deportation; and fired a shotgun over their heads in order to prevent the workers from attempting escape.

From an indigenous community in San Luis Potosí, the workers were recruited in Mexico by Relan and allegedly forced to pick strawberries in Amite from 2006 to 2008. Many of the workers spoke Nahuatl as their first language and spoke basic Spanish but little to no English. According to the complaint against Bimbo's Best Produce, Relan "subjected the guest workers to a scheme of psychological coercion, threats of serious harm, and threatened abuse of the legal process to maintain control over them and force them to continue working in his strawberry fields."

As stated in the complaint, Relan regularly berated the workers and at times informed them that they were to stay in the bent position of tending to the strawberry plants rather than being allowed to stand up. The complaint goes on to state that he physically assaulted at least one worker, plaintiff Reynaldo Reyes-Resendiz. Allegedly, Relan yelled at Reynaldo and accused him of weeding the strawberry plants incorrectly. When Reynaldo tried to continue working, Relan allegedly shoved him.

According to the complaint, Relan frequently carried a gun in the strawberry fields and on occasion would shoot above the workers' heads. One day, the Bimbo's owner allegedly decided to shoot and kill a neighbor's dog—a dog that the workers had befriended. The execution of the dog took place in the same area where the victims were working, which made them more fearful that they could be harmed.

The complaint also states that pesticides were sprayed in the direct vicinity of the laborers while they worked. As a result, the spray and vapor came into immediate contact with the workers' mouths and skin, which in legal terms constitutes a harmful and offensive contact to the victims. . . .

An Alliance for Gulf Coast Guest Workers

In response to their own exploitative experiences in the Gulf Coast, a number of guest workers have joined together with the NOWCRJ [New Orleans Workers' Center for Racial Justice] to create an association called the Alliance of Guestworkers for Dignity. Started in January 2007, the New Orleans–based coalition is led by H-2B guest workers whose objective is to advocate for the fair treatment of workers. It also aims to bring attention to guest worker exploitation and the occurrence of debt bondage and indentured servitude that has resulted from lax enforcement of labor law. Among other nations, members are from Mexico, Peru, Brazil, Bolivia, and India.

New US Immigrants at Risk of Becoming Forced Labor Victims

Kira Zalan

Kira Zalan is an editor for U.S. News Weekly *and a freelance journalist.*

In the following viewpoint, Zalan discusses the little-acknowledged problem of forced labor in the United States. Zalan points out that there are millions of forced labor victims around the world, and many of these victims can be found in the United States. In America, the most vulnerable population of becoming forced labor victims are new immigrants. Zalan explains that many victims are lured to the United States by false promises. They often have their documentation confiscated. Because of new immigrants' unfamiliarity with US laws and customs, they are often reluctant to ask for help.

Ima Matul sat under the bright examination light in a Los Angeles hospital, while an emergency room doctor stared suspiciously at the wound on her head. She wondered if the doctor could really see her brain, like her employer said he could when he first saw the wound. "Tell them that you fell in the backyard and bumped your head on a rock," she recalls being told as a condition of being taken to the hospital to get stitches. Now, the doctor was saying something she didn't understand in English, and her employer was answering for her. Ima, an Indonesian national, knew the employer probably wasn't telling the truth, that it was his wife who had split Ima's head open that morning during another rage-filled ti-

Kira Zalan, "Emerging from the Shadows," *U.S. News Weekly,* March 29, 2013, pp. 11–14. Copyright © 2013 by U.S. News & World Report. All rights reserved. Reproduced by permission.

rade about her cleaning skills. By then, Ima had endured two years of emotional and physical abuse, while working in the family's home without pay.

Soon after that incident, Ima wrote a plea in her limited English on a piece of paper: "Please help me. I cannot take it anymore." She kept it hidden for months before overcoming her fear and handing the note to a nanny who worked next door. The nanny told her employer, who then contacted the Coalition to Abolish Slavery & Trafficking [CAST], which would arrange Ima's desperate escape a few days later. While the family slept, Ima snuck out of the house and ran to a get-away car waiting down the street, carrying a small bag of clothes she had brought from Indonesia.

Forced Labor Is a Worldwide Problem

An estimated 21 million people are subjected to forced labor worldwide, according to the International Labour Organization. In the United States, American citizens and foreign nationals are trafficked—subjected to forced labor, debt bondage and involuntary servitude through the use of force, fraud or coercion—in brothels and factories, in hotels and restaurants, on farms and in homes. In a speech where he acknowledged how widespread the problem is, President [Barack] Obama called human trafficking "modern slavery" and announced additional anti-trafficking efforts in September [2012]. But despite increased efforts by the administration, service providers worry that stronger enforcement of immigration laws is keeping foreign victims silent.

Foreign nationals that become trafficking victims in the United States, like Ima, have a commonly exploited vulnerability: their immigration status. Victims' advocacy groups say increased immigration enforcement has had a chilling effect on anti-trafficking efforts by fostering a climate of fear among the most vulnerable immigrant populations.

New Immigrants Are at Risk in the United States

While there are as many different narratives as there are traf-ficking cases, Ima's tale is a familiar one, experts say. She was 16 years old and living in her native Indonesia when she heard about the job opportunity—working as a nanny for a family in Los Angeles. The $150 monthly salary she was promised would be enough to support her parents and two younger sib-lings back home. Millions of Indonesians leave home to work abroad, mostly in Asia and the Middle East, sending home re-mittances. Ima's recruiter arranged her passport, visa and transportation to Los Angeles. Ima didn't know that the tour-ist visa she traveled on meant that working in the United States was illegal.

The first week in America, Ima and her cousin, who also came in search of work, stayed in a transition house, learning which American brand cleaning products to use on which surfaces. Then the woman who would be Ima's employer, an interior designer married to a businessman, picked her up. Soon after Ima began her job as a nanny, the conditions changed. She was made to work 18-hour days, seven days a week, without pay. When Ima was caught trying to send a let-ter to her cousin, who was placed to work in another Los An-geles home, the employer began to physically abuse her and said she'd be arrested or worse if she tried to leave.

Ima didn't know her visa status or American laws. She had no one to turn to and didn't speak English. She believed the threats.

The threat of arrest and deportation is a common tool traffickers use to control their victims, experts say. Often, they'll confiscate the victim's immigration documents, as Ima's employer did. In another case, last November, the Justice De-partment secured a life sentence in the conviction of Alex Campbell, a 45-year-old massage parlor owner in suburban Il-linois. Besides using violence to coerce three women from

Ukraine and one woman from Belarus into forced labor and commercial sex, he had confiscated their passports and visas. At the trial, prosecutors showed that Campbell targeted foreign women without legal status in the United States. Ima's traffickers were never prosecuted.

But even those immigrants who arrive on a legitimate work-related visa have become trafficking victims. These visas usually bind the worker to an employer, who can hold that requirement over their head and even become their trafficker. "If employment ends, then so does visa status," says Avaloy Lanning, senior director of the anti-trafficking program at Safe Horizon, a New York–based victims' services agency. "The trafficker uses that against them, [saying], if you run then you're going to be illegal, then immigration is going to pick you up, arrest you and deport you." Because of the vulnerability for exploitation and abuse this creates, victims' advocates are now pushing for comprehensive reform of the temporary worker program to be included in the anticipated immigration legislation.

Many Trafficking Victims Too Fearful to Ask for Help

While there are no reliable numbers to gauge the full scope of human trafficking in the United States, Immigration and Customs Enforcement's [ICE's] Homeland Security Investigations directorate in fiscal 2012 initiated 894 human trafficking investigations, made 967 arrests and 559 indictments, and secured 381 convictions. The Federal Bureau of Investigation had about 450 pending human trafficking investigations at the end of last year. The National Human Trafficking Resource Center, a hotline funded in part by the federal government and operated by the nonprofit Polaris Project, received 20,639 calls last year, referencing 2,333 potential victims—1,367 of them placed by potentially trafficked persons. Forty-one percent of calls received in past years referenced foreign nationals, 43 percent referenced U.S. citizens, and the rest were un-known. In 2004, the last time such an estimate was made, the federal government estimated that between 14,500 and 17,500 people were trafficked into the United States. According to the State Department, most foreign victims identified in 2011 came from Mexico, the Philippines, Thailand, Guatemala, Honduras and India.

In 2000, Congress passed landmark legislation called the Trafficking Victims Protection Act, which, among other things, authorized the government to provide temporary immigration relief for foreign victims. In recent years, the Department of Homeland Security [DHS] and other agencies have launched global, national and local outreach campaigns to inform vulnerable communities about their rights. More federal, state and local law enforcement officials are being trained in recognizing signs of trafficking and taking on a victim-centered approach. "No matter where a person's from or what their immigration status is, they should come forward to law enforcement," says Angie Salazar, who is in charge of ICE's smuggling and trafficking division. "We will always investigate a case; and, if they are identified as a victim of human trafficking, they have rights under the law regardless."

Still, law enforcement officials say most trafficking victims are identified through nonprofit and local service providers. Increased enforcement, including the deportation of more than almost 1.6 million people since 2009, has made it less likely that victims will come forward, service providers say.

"There is a heightened resistance among exploited immigrants to seek protection from law enforcement, to access social services and health care, or to seek assistance related to exploitation or violations of legal rights," states a policy paper published by Freedom Network USA, a national alliance of 30 anti-trafficking organizations. "Any effort to reach out for help brings a risk of disclosure of their lack of status and related immigration enforcement measures. The resulting detention, even if minimal, reinforces the exploitative employer's threats of law enforcement and the immigration system."

"If our government's perceived [to have] these increased enforcement schemes, the traffickers will essentially have a point," says Ivy Suriyopas, policy co-chair at Freedom Network and head of the anti-trafficking initiative at the Asian American Legal Defense and Education Fund. "Immigrant victims are not going to come forward if they fear that the NYPD [New York City Police Department] or the LAPD [Los Angeles Police Department] are not going to come help them but might label them a criminal first and ask questions later. Or maybe never ask questions at all."

Tiffany Williams, advocacy director for the Institute for Policy Studies' Break the Chain Campaign, a D.C.-based migrant workers' rights organization that's also part of Freedom Network, says she and other social workers are seeing "more fear and reluctance" about coming forward, particularly in states with aggressive immigration enforcement laws, like Arizona and Georgia, and since the expansion of the Secure Communities initiative, a federal fingerprinting program to identify undocumented immigrants. "What we've seen on the ground is that the more aggressive they are with these [enforcement] programs, where they're allowing local police to arrest people for being undocumented, the more that the Secure Communities programs and others are growing, the less likely it is that an immigrant survivor would be willing to come forward and ask for help," Williams says, referring to victims of trafficking and other crimes. "It impedes our work significantly," she adds.

More immigrants have been deported since 2009 than during eight years of the [George W.] Bush administration. In 2012, the Obama administration spent 24 percent more on immigration enforcement agencies than on all other federal law enforcement agencies combined, according to the Migration Policy Institute. The Secure Communities program, which began in 2008 by offering states and localities voluntary participation, has become mandatory. At the end of last year, ICE had 39 agreements with local law enforcement agencies in 19 states, delegating federal immigration enforcement authority to them.

More Needs to Be Done to Help Trafficking Victims

The consequences are detrimental to both immigrant communities and law enforcement, victims' advocates say. "I know it's true from talking to people from immigrant communities and from talking to law enforcement [officers] who aren't really supportive of acting in this way. Because if we're talking about the NYPD or the Dallas Police Department or whoever that has to go into immigrant communities to investigate crime, they can say, 'I'm not immigration, I'm not here to deport you . . . I'm here to hear about what's happened to you, to make it better; there's justice for you.' And if they had to act as an arm of immigration, they couldn't say that anymore, and they would lose the trust of those immigrant communities," says Lanning.

Alongside the growing mandate to enforce immigration regulations, law enforcement agencies are increasingly trained to deal with trafficking cases. "We have to ensure that if someone is here illegally that we uphold the law and do whatever it takes to ensure that we are fair to that person," says Salazar, the DHS official. "Depending on why we've intercepted them, different courses of action can happen. But when it comes to human trafficking investigations, and any of the investigations we do when there's a human being at the center of our investigation, they are of the utmost priority, regardless of their immigration status." Salazar doesn't think the agency's dual mandates are at odds, but admits there is a challenge. Getting victims to come forward, she says, "is a challenge for law enforcement in general. Probably a little more [for us] because we are an immigration law enforcement agency. But a lot of these victims come from these countries where corrupt law enforcement is common," she says, referring to many immigrants' inherent lack of trust of law enforcement.

Traffickers range from opportunistic individuals to criminal organizations to employment recruiting companies, experts say. Victims don't fit a single profile, varying in gender, age, education level, origin and other factors. The control exercised over a victim by a trafficker is sometimes physical and always psychological. "Many times the trafficker is keeping them in a state of limbo and hope that this will somehow get better if they just comply with a set of demands or requirements or obligations," says Gary Haugen, a former Justice Department official and founder of International Justice Mission, a U.S.-based nonprofit that rescues victims of trafficking and violence overseas. "And so the victim is frequently trying to calculate, 'Okay, am I going to get out of this situation by maybe just doing the next thing that's asked of me—pay a little more money, do this thing I tell you, don't make me mad—or do I really try to go against my trafficker and seek outside help?' "

Service providers are rooting for immigration reforms that might make the choice of seeking help more viable. Removing the trafficker's ability to hold a victim's immigration status over their head would arm them with the ability to complain about working conditions, to change employers, or come to a social service agency without fear of being arrested, Williams says.

Ima now works as a survivor organizer for CAST, the Los Angeles organization that rescued her. She has met President Obama and testified before Congress on human trafficking.

Child Sex Slaves in America

Malika Saada Saar

Malika Saada Saar is special counsel on human rights at the Raben Group and director of the Human Rights Project for Girls. She has been named one of the 150 women who shake the world by Newsweek *magazine.*

In the following viewpoint, Saar looks at the state of child sex trafficking in America. The statistics collected by Rights4Girls show that most girls who are held and trafficked for sex are between the ages of twelve and fourteen and most are US citizens. The majority come from broken homes and the broken foster care system. It is, Saar writes, more profitable to make money from a young girl than from drugs, yet the government spends three hundred times more money fighting drugs than fighting child sex slavery. Most of these children, unlike agricultural slaves, are out in public places where ordinary citizens see them every day. They are slaves in the sense that they are forced into sex labor, their money goes to their handlers, and they are tortured or gang-raped if they try to run away. These children, instead of being protected, are viewed as criminals, and their handlers are rarely prosecuted.

On the 150th anniversary of when President [Abraham] Lincoln issued the preliminary Emancipation Proclamation, which set the date for the freedom of more than 3 million enslaved Americans, President Obama called for the end of modern-day slavery.

The Call for an End to Slavery

The president's historical speech delivered at the Clinton Global Initiative, called for major policy changes, at home and abroad, to combat the enslavement of millions of women, men and children.

Malika Saada Saar, "Girls, Human Trafficking, and Modern Slavery in America," *Think-Progress*, October 6, 2012. Copyright © 2012 by Malika Saada Saar. All rights reserved. Reproduced by permission.

Many of the slaves today are girls. Born in America. Hidden in plain view.

They are the lost girls, standing around bus stops, hanging out by runaway youth shelters, or advertised online. At the Motel 8 or the Marriott, at McDonalds or the clubs.

The Enormity of Sexual Trafficking of Children

According to the FBI [Federal Bureau of Investigation], there are currently an estimated 293,000 American children at risk of being exploited and trafficked for sex. Forty percent of all human trafficking cases opened for investigation between January 2008 and June 2010 were for the sexual trafficking of a child. And while the term trafficking may conjure images of desperate illegal immigrants being forced into prostitution by human smugglers, 83 percent of victims in confirmed sex trafficking cases in this country were American citizens.

The majority of these children being sold for sex are girls between the ages of 12 and 14. They are girls abducted or lured by traffickers and then routinely raped, beaten into submission, and sometimes even branded. When the girls try to run away, their traffickers torture and or gang-rape them.

They are girls like Jackie who ran away from an abusive home at 13 only to be found alone and hungry by a trafficker who promised to love her like a father/boyfriend/Prince Charming. He sold her to at least six different men every night. When she begged him for food or rest, he beat her.

More Lucrative than Drugs

Young girls like Jackie are the new commodities that traffickers and gangs are selling. In many respects, the girl trade has replaced the drug trade. Drug routes have been repurposed to sell girls, along I-95, and up and down the I-5 corridor. The emergence of the Internet also allows the sale of a girl to be executed with ease, discretion, and convenience for the buyer. And unlike selling a drug, the girl is "reusable."

Child sex trafficking exists in the United States. Experts say that most girls who are held captive and trafficked for sex are between the ages of twelve and fourteen. © UIG via Getty Images.

The ugly truth is that it is less risky and more profitable to sell a girl than crack cocaine or meth. The U.S. government spends 300 times more money each year to fight drug trafficking than it does to fight human trafficking. And the criminal penalties for drug trafficking are generally greater than the ones usually levied against those who traffic in girls. Traffickers, and especially the politely termed "Johns," are rarely arrested and prosecuted. Which explains the growing demand for very young girls—at the click of a mouse, a "John" can purchase a girl online on legitimate websites like Backpage .com, with minimal fear of punishment.

Broken Foster Care System

Many of these girls who are bought and sold for sex come out of a broken foster care system. Of the trafficking victims in Alameda County, California, 55 percent were from foster youth group homes. In New York, 85 percent of trafficking victims had prior child welfare involvement. And in Florida, the head of the state's trafficking task force estimates that 70 percent of victims are foster youth.

"T" was born into the foster care system and trafficked at the age of 10, sold to men all over California, Washington, Oregon and Nevada. She recently shared her own observation at a congressional briefing on how foster care rendered her vulnerable to being exploited. "In most of my 14 different placements in foster care homes, I was raped, and attached to a check. I understood very early that I could be raped, cared for, and connected to money. It was therefore easy to go from that to a pimp, and at least the pimp told me that he loved me."

Unfortunately, most child welfare systems have failed to properly identify and assist trafficked and exploited children. The protections, services, and protocols established for abused and neglected children within the child welfare system are rarely extended to trafficked girls. Instead, the girls are relegated to the juvenile justice system, criminalized for being raped and trafficked. This must be the only time in which it is the abused child . . . who is incarcerated for the abuse perpetrated against her.

But that's the problem—these girls are not considered victims. So while in the United States, we have the very same child sex slave markets as in Cambodia, the Philippines, and India, the girls from here, the girls from Southeast DC or South Central LA, are seen as the "ho," the bad girl, the teen hooker.

It is time to really see these girls and help them. This is the moment to heed President Obama's call to end modern-day slavery, and let's start right here at home. Because no girl in America, in the 21st century, should be for sale.

Research Can Aid in Understanding and Preventing Modern-Day Slavery in the United States

Maureen Q. McGough

Maureen Q. McGough is an attorney and international research partnership specialist in the National Institute of Justice's Office of Research Partnerships.

In the following viewpoint, McGough discusses some of the challenges of grasping the scope of modern-day slavery. Captors prey on individuals with little visibility and keep their victims hidden. McGough discusses recent research aimed at combating human trafficking. The goal of this research is to gain a better understanding of the nature and prevalence of human trafficking as well as how to improve legal enforcement to better prosecute those who engage in various forms of modern-day slavery.

Trafficking in persons is modern-day slavery and exists in virtually every country in the world—and the United States is no exception. Almost 150 years after the 13th Amendment abolished slavery and involuntary servitude, there are still men, women and children enslaved into labor and commercial sexual exploitation in the U.S. . . .

A Hidden Crime

The nature of human trafficking helps keep this crime hidden. Captors often closely guard their victims, leaving them isolated with little to no freedom of movement. They restrict victims' contact with the outside world. Domestic servants re-

Maureen Q. McGough, "Ending Modern-Day Slavery: Using Research to Inform U.S. Anti-Human Trafficking Efforts," *NIJ Journal*, February 2013. Reproduced by permission.

main "invisible" in private homes, and private businesses can serve as fronts for trafficking operations. Many victims face language barriers that prevent them from seeking help. Additionally, international victims who enter the U.S. may be uncertain of their immigration status and thus less inclined to work with authorities.

Furthermore, victims, for a variety of reasons, do not always identify themselves as such. Human trafficking victims suffer tragic psychological trauma and may experience Stockholm syndrome, generating positive feelings and gratitude toward their captors for perceived favors or even for being allowed to live. Law enforcement commonly lacks training to identify these signs of trauma, making it difficult for them to sever the controlling bond that captors have over their victims and decreasing the likelihood that victims will cooperate. Even if victims identify themselves as such and are aware of their rights, they still might hesitate to report their victimization out of fear of reprisal from the trafficker, lack of trust in law enforcement or fear of deportation.

Challenges at the State and Local Levels

Since the passage of the Trafficking Victims Protection Act in 2000, 49 states have enacted legislation that criminalizes human trafficking and empowers state and local law enforcement—often the first responders to interact with victims—to investigate these cases without depending on federal authorities and to prosecute human trafficking cases in state courts.

Increased involvement of state and local law enforcement is critical because they handle the bulk of criminal cases in the United States. Even before the passage of state anti-trafficking legislation, federal law enforcement requested that state and local officers "be the eyes and ears for [federal law enforcement in] recognizing, uncovering and responding to circumstances that may appear to be routine street crime, but may ultimately turn out to be a human trafficking case." In fact, in a survey of state and local law enforcement personnel, 32 percent of respondents indicated that they identified many of their human trafficking cases when they were investigating other crimes.

Despite this increased involvement, reports show that fewer trafficking cases have been identified and prosecuted than would be expected given current estimates. This has led to speculation that either incidents of human trafficking are significantly overestimated or government officials and law enforcement agencies are not effectively confronting the problem.

NIJ [National Institute of Justice] funded Amy Farrell and her colleagues at Northeastern University and researchers at the Urban Institute to examine the challenges facing state and local criminal justice systems when investigating and prosecuting human trafficking cases. The researchers conducted a 12-site study that included in-depth interviews with 166 practitioners from federal, state and local law enforcement; state and federal prosecutors; victim service providers; and other stakeholders. The researchers also analyzed data from 140 closed human trafficking case files to determine which characteristics of human trafficking cases attract local law enforcement's attention and predict adjudicatory outcomes. Although the study is not nationally representative, the findings can help us understand why the number of human trafficking cases is lower than estimates of the problem might predict. Here is what the researchers found.

Identification Challenges

The study confirmed that identifying victims is particularly challenging because perpetrators hide and move their victims. The interviews also revealed that the cultural and organizational characteristics of police agencies can hinder efforts to identify victims and that local law enforcement and communities generally do not make combating human trafficking a priority. This often means fewer resources for training and staff for labor-intensive investigations.

The cases the researchers reviewed had primarily been identified through reactive approaches, illustrating that officers generally wait for victims to self-identify or for community tips about potential victimization to be received before they launch investigations. The researchers found that law enforcement uniformly lamented the lack of identified labor trafficking cases, suggesting that although officers believe labor trafficking is occurring in local communities, they have not received information about these cases. The use of proactive strategies to identify trafficking cases was uncommon and rarely involved cooperation between law enforcement and prosecutors.

Investigation Challenges

Researchers in the Northeastern University/Urban Institute study reviewed 140 closed trafficking case files to determine whether the evidence supported a charge of human trafficking as outlined in the Trafficking Victims Protection Act and its reauthorizations. The review found evidence of human trafficking in the majority of the cases. Among the indicators found were threatening to harm or actually physically or non-physically harming the victim; demeaning and demoralizing the victim; dominating, intimidating and controlling the victim; and disorienting and depriving the victim of alternatives. However, few suspects were actually charged with human trafficking offenses. Even when they received specific human trafficking cases, prosecutors were more likely to prosecute using laws with which they, judges and juries were more familiar, such as promoting prostitution, kidnapping or fraud.

Interviews with practitioners confirmed what other research has shown: Victims were reluctant to cooperate with investigations because they either feared retaliation from their trafficker or distrusted law enforcement. In some cases, be-

President George W. Bush, center, is applauded by Homeland Security Secretary Michael Chertoff, left, and Attorney General Michael Mukasey, right, and lawmakers after he signed the Trafficking Victims Protection Reauthorization Act of 2008. © ASSOCIATED PRESS.

cause jurisdictions lacked specialized services for trafficking victims, such as secure housing, law enforcement officers arrested victims to keep them from returning to their traffickers or to help them feel safe from pimps and thereby encourage the victims' cooperation in the investigation. Although the arrest was often for the victim's protection, it essentially resulted in the victim being treated like a suspect. These victims may feel re-victimized and experience the same negative emotions they experienced in the trafficking situation, thus adding to often preexisting distrust of law enforcement.

Specialized services for trafficking victims are all the more critical because victims' loyalty to their traffickers may stem, in part, from feelings that they have no practical alternatives to their current situation.

One of the law enforcement practitioners interviewed explained the potential impact that additional resources could have on combating trafficking by providing victims with a viable alternative:

We have nothing to say, "Hey, I can put you up in . . . this place. And I can help you get an education. And I can help you get a job. And I can help you take care of your kids." You know, we don't have that. If I had that, man . . . we could stop prostitution.

Interviews with law enforcement officers also revealed that some officers had negative stereotypes about the people commonly found to be victims of human trafficking, especially those involved with prostitution and those with drug addictions. Some reported the use of derogatory terms for victims, and one officer said, "Victims are often unreliable, often addicted to drugs. It's probably easier to prosecute homicides because the victims are dead."

Law enforcement commonly lacked training on how to investigate human trafficking cases. The researchers found that in many study sites, vice investigators were conducting human trafficking investigations using standard vice investigation strategies geared toward drug and gambling crimes, further reducing the likelihood of a successful trafficking investigation.

Additionally, many trafficking cases are cross-jurisdictional, and agencies reported that cases often fell apart when they lacked the resources or institutional support to gather evidence or conduct interviews in other states. Importantly, officers indicated that they could not dedicate time and resources to investigate cases they felt would not result in prosecution.

Therefore, the reluctance of prosecutors to file charges in human trafficking cases created a negative feedback loop, in some instances diminishing an investigator's determination to identify and investigate these challenging cases.

Prosecution Challenges

Because state statutes on human trafficking are relatively new, there is a lack of precedent and case law, and prosecutors operate with little or no guidance on prosecutorial techniques or other resources, such as sample jury instructions. Many prosecutors interviewed in the study by Farrell and colleagues said they were concerned about losing high-profile cases (and damaging their reputation), and so they prosecuted cases using a charge other than human trafficking. A local prosecutor said, "[T]hat was sort of the unwritten policy of the office: 'Why bother with this goofy human trafficking statute, just charge other crimes that you are more comfortable with and that you have used in the past.'" Prosecutors also reported that victims were often reluctant to testify or did not seem credible, and most state and local agencies lacked the institutional infrastructure (such as a specialized human trafficking unit) to support prosecution.

Although few of the cases studied resulted in suspects being charged for human trafficking offenses, offenders were held accountable in 69 percent of the cases, in that they were prosecuted for different offenses, such as rape, kidnapping or pandering. However, this poses an obvious problem in crime reporting. For example, the 2008 reauthorization of the Trafficking Victims Protection Act mandates that the FBI collect information about human trafficking offenses through the Uniform Crime Reporting (UCR) program. But unless state and local law enforcement routinely investigate human trafficking cases as such, crime data reported through the UCR will inevitably undercount instances of human trafficking. Underreporting could be more harmful than no reporting at all, particularly when agencies tie funding decisions to what the crime data show are the most prevalent problems.

The Road Ahead

Human trafficking is believed to be a growing crime, fueled by low risk and the potential for high monetary gain. Although we still need reliable estimates of nationwide prevalence, it is clear that human trafficking occurs on a large scale within U.S. borders.

For Further Discussion

1. Follow the course of Frederick Douglass's developing literacy. For what reasons, do you suspect, were slaves forbidden to learn to read? Reread the viewpoint by Russell K. Hively to inform your answer.

2. For what reasons were even Sunday school classes prohibited for slaves? Give some hypothetical examples to illustrate your view. Reread the viewpoint by Frederick Douglass and Robert G. O'Meally to inform your answer.

3. Discuss the irony of the slave owners' religion and Douglass's argument in his appendix in *Narrative of the Life of Frederick Douglass*. Can you think of contemporary examples of his argument? Use information found in the viewpoints by Robert G. O'Meally, Scott C. Williamson, and Donald B. Gibson to formulate your response.

4. Why were slaveholders determined to split up families? Reread viewpoints by Wu Jin-Ping and Henry Louis Gates Jr. to inform your answer.

5. Discuss the difficulties Douglass encountered in the North. Reread viewpoints by Houston A. Baker Jr. and Frederick Douglass.

6. How did Douglass attempt to establish an identity? Reread viewpoints by Wu Jin-Ping, Philip S. Foner, and Henry Louis Gates Jr. to formulate your response.

For Further Reading

William Wells Brown, *Narrative of William Wells Brown, a Fugitive Slave; Written by Himself.* Boston, MA: The Anti-Slavery Office, 1847.

Mary Chesnut, *A Diary from Dixie.* Ed. Ben Ames Williams. Cambridge, MA: Harvard University Press, 1980.

Frederick Douglass, *The Frederick Douglass Papers: Series One: Speeches, Debates, and Interviews.* Ed. John W. Blassingame et al. New Haven, CT: Yale University Press, 1979.

———, *The Life and Times of Frederick Douglass, Written by Himself.* Hertfordshire: Wordsworth Editions, 1996.

———, *My Bondage and My Freedom.* Ed. John David Smith. New York: Penguin Books, 2003.

Henry Goings, *Rambles of a Runaway from Southern Slavery.* Ed. Calvin Schermerhorn, Michael Plunkett, and Edward Gaynor. Charlottesville: University of Virginia Press, 2012.

Harriet Jacobs, *Incidents in the Life of a Slave Girl.* New York: W.W. Norton, 2001.

Frances Anne Kemble, *Journal of a Residence on a Georgia Plantation in 1838–1839.* Savannah: Library of Georgia, 1992.

Solomon Northup, *Twelve Years a Slave.* New York: Penguin Books, 2012.

Harriet Beecher Stowe, *Uncle Tom's Cabin.* Boston, MA: John P. Jewett, 1852.

Bibliography

Books

Kevin Bales and
Zoe Trodd, eds.

To Plead Our Cause: Personal Stories by Today's Slaves. Ithaca, NY: Cornell University Press, 2008.

David W. Blight

Frederick Douglass' Civil War: Keeping Faith in Jubilee. Baton Rouge: Louisiana State University Press, 1989.

Free the Slaves
and Human
Rights Center

Hidden Slaves: Forced Labor in the United States. Washington, DC: Free the Slaves, 2005.

Frederic May
Holland

Frederick Douglass: The Colored Orator. Westport, CT: Negro Universities Press, 1970.

Nathan Irvin
Huggins

Slave and Citizen: The Life of Frederick Douglass. Ed. Oscar Handlin. Boston: Little, Brown and Company, 1980.

Aileen S. Kraditor

Means and Ends in American Abolitionism: Garrison and His Critics on Strategy and Tactics, 1834–1850. New York: Pantheon, 1969.

George P. Lampe

Frederick Douglass: Freedom's Voice 1818–1845. East Lansing: Michigan State University Press, 1998.

Bill E. Lawson and Frank M. Kirkland, eds.	*Frederick Douglass: A Critical Reader.* Malden, MA: Blackwell Publishers, 1999.
Waldo E. Martin Jr.	*The Mind of Frederick Douglass.* Chapel Hill: University of North Carolina Press, 1984.
Charles H. Nichols	*Many Thousand Gone: The Ex-Slaves' Account of Their Bondage and Freedom.* Bloomington: Indiana University Press, 1963.
Dickson J. Preston	*Young Frederick Douglass: The Maryland Years.* Baltimore, MD: Johns Hopkins University Press, 1980.
Benjamin Quarles	*Frederick Douglass.* Washington, DC: Associated Publishers, 1968.
Joel Quirk	*The Anti-Slavery Project: From the Slave Trade to Human Trafficking.* Philadelphia: University of Pennsylvania Press, 2011.
Valerie Smith	*Self-Discovery and Authority in Afro-American Narrative.* Cambridge, MA: Harvard University Press, 1987.
Petrus C. van Duyne and Jon Spencer	*Flesh and Money: Trafficking in Human Beings.* The Netherlands: Wolf Legan Publishers, 2011.

Periodicals

William L. Andrews	"Frederick Douglass, Preacher," *American Literature,* vol. 54, no. 4, December 1982, pp. 592–596.

John W.
Blassingame

"Black Autobiographies as History and Literature," *Black Scholar*, vol. 5, no. 4, December 1973–January 1974, pp. 2–9.

David W. Blight

"Frederick Douglass and the American Apocalypse," *Civil War History*, vol. 31, no. 4, December 1985, pp. 309–328.

Christopher N.
Breiseth

"Lincoln and Frederick Douglass: Another Debate," *Journal of the Illinois State Historical Society*, vol. 68, no. 1, February 1975, pp. 9–26.

Frederick Cooper

"Elevating the Race: The Social Thought of Black Leaders, 1827–1850," *American Quarterly*, vol. 24, December 1972, pp. 604–625.

Gerald Fulkerson

"Exile as Emergence: Frederick Douglass in Great Britain, 1845–1847," *Quarterly Journal of Speech*, vol. 60, no. 1, February 1974, pp. 69–82.

Henry Louis
Gates Jr.

"Binary Oppositions in Chapter One of *Narrative of the Life of Frederick Douglass, an American Slave Narrative Written by Himself*," *Afro-American Literature: The Reconstruction of Instruction*. Ed. Dexter Fisher and Robert B. Stepto. New York: Modern Language Association, 1979.

Henry Louis
Gates Jr.
"Frederick Douglass and the
Language of the Self," *Yale Review*,
Summer 1981, pp. 592–611.

Leslie Friedman
Goldstein
"Violence as an Instrument for Social
Change: The Views of Frederick
Douglass," *Journal of Negro History*,
vol. 61, no. 1, January 1976, pp.
61–72.

Francis J. Grimke
"The Second Marriage of Frederick
Douglass," *Journal of Negro History*,
vol. 19, no. 3, July 1934, pp. 324–329.

David
Howard-Pitney
"The Enduring Black Jeremiad: The
American Jeremiad and Black Protest
Rhetoric, from Frederick Douglass to
W.E.B. DuBois, 1841–1919," *American
Quarterly*, vol. 38, no. 3, 1986, pp.
481–492.

August Meier
"Frederick Douglass' Vision for
America: A Case Study in Nineteenth
Century Protest," *Freedom and
Reform: Essays in Honor of Henry
Steele Commager.* Ed. Harold M.
Hyman and Leonard W. Levy. New
York: Harper and Row, 1967, pp.
127–148.

Jane H. Pease and
William H. Pease
"Boston Garrisonians and the
Problem of Frederick Douglass,"
Canadian Journal of History, vol. 2,
no. 2, September 1967, pp. 27–48.

Kirk Semple "Housekeeper in New Jersey Accuses Peruvian Diplomat of Human Trafficking," *New York Times*, June 25, 2013.

George Shepperson "Frederick Douglass and Scotland." *Journal of Negro History*, vol. 38, no. 3, July 1953, pp. 307–321.

Robert B. Stepto "Narration, Authentication, and Authorial Control in Frederick Douglass' *Narrative* of 1845," *Afro-American Literature: The Reconstruction of Instruction*. Ed. Dexter Fisher and Robert B. Stepto. New York: Modern Language Association, 1979.

Albert E. Stone "Identity and Art in Frederick Douglass' *Narrative*," *CLA Journal*, vol. 17, 1973, pp. 192–213.

US Department of Education "Human Trafficking of Children in the United States: A Fact Sheet for Schools," June 2007. www.ed.gov /about/offices/list/isdfs/Factsheet.

William L. Van DeBurg "Frederick Douglass: Maryland Slave to Religious Liberal," *Maryland Historical Magazine*, vol. 69, Spring 1974, pp. 27–43.

Stephen M. Weisman "Frederick Douglass, Portrait of a Black Militant: A Study in Family Romance," *Psychoanalytic Study of the Child*, vol. 30, 1975, pp. 725–751.

Joy M. Zarembka "America's Dirty Work: Migrant
Maids and Modern-Day Slavery,"
*Global Woman: Nannies, Maids, and
Sex Workers in the New Economy.* Ed.
Barbara Ehrenreich and Arlie Russell
Hochschild. New York: Metropolitan
Books, 2002, pp. 142–153.

Index